Kahoot!
QUIZ TIME
EARTH

Written by
Rona Skene

DK

Contents

Introduction

How old is our planet? Which place has had no rain for 14 million years? How much does a cloud weigh? Test your knowledge of Earth with these quizzes, packed with quirky questions and fun facts.

Explore every part of the world, from the driest deserts and the soggiest swamps to the busiest cities and deepest, darkest ocean depths. What on Earth are you waiting for? Let's get started!

Keep score

Most quizzes in this book have 10 questions each. To keep score, you'll need to record the number of correct answers each player gets after each quiz.

Keep track on a piece of paper or even on a spreadsheet. Be sure to tally up the score for each quiz in order to crown the ultimate winner based on who gets the highest score from all 30 quizzes. Who will grab the gold medal?

Find more quizzes!

Look for QR codes throughout the book. Scan them to find exclusive online quizzes on the same theme. You can also head over to www.kahoot.com to discover more than 100 million quizzes on loads of interesting subjects!

Find 15 QR codes like this one on the pages that follow.

Make your own

Once you've completed these quizzes, get inspired to create your own on kahoot.com!

First, plan out your questions on paper and check out our tips to make your quiz the best it can be. When it's ready, share your quiz with friends and family.

Don't worry about who wins or if your quiz doesn't turn out exactly how you planned. The important thing is to have fun . . . but it's even more important to stay safe online. Never share any personal information with anyone online and always use the internet with a trusted adult.

Tips

1 Do your research and always check your facts with three trusted online sources.

2 Give your quiz a fun theme and vary your questions so the quiz doesn't get repetitive.

3 Include three or four multiple choice options, plus a few true or false and picture rounds.

Planet Earth

Let's take a close-up look at this watery, airy, spinning sphere of rock we Earthlings call home!

1 Roughly how old is Earth?
- ◆ 700 million years
- ▲ 4.5 billion years
- ● 37 billion years

2 Which planet is nearest to Earth?
- ◆ Venus
- ▲ The moon
- ● The sun

3 How long does it take for Earth to make one complete spin?
- ◆ One day
- ▲ One month
- ● One year

4 Put these life-forms in the order they first appeared on Earth:
- ◆ Mammals
- ▲ Fish
- ● Bacteria

Did you know?

NASA scientists estimate that there are up to 300 million Earth-like planets in our galaxy with the conditions needed for life to survive!

5 300 million years ago, Earth had one giant ocean and a single supercontinent called...
- ◆ Permia
- ▲ Pangea
- ● Protozoa

6 Earth's inner core is mostly made of which metal?

◆ Gold
▲ Iron
● Steel

7 Earth's crust floats above a layer of hot rock called...

◆ The mantle
▲ The outer core
● The magma zone

8 During which of Earth's geological eras did the dinosaurs first appear?

◆ Mesozoic Era
▲ Paleozoic Era
● Cenozoic Era

9 What causes this natural light show in Earth's polar regions?

◆ Super-powerful thunderstorms
▲ The moon's gravity
● Charged particles from the sun

10 What caused the dinosaurs to become extinct—probably?

◆ A COVID-like virus
▲ Asteroid strike on Earth
● Human hunters

Turn to page 8 for the answers!

Planet Earth
Answers

1 **Roughly how old is Earth?**

▲ 4.5 billion years

Scientists believe Earth formed when gravity forced clouds of dust and gas together creating rocks—gradually one grew into Earth.

2 **Which planet is nearest to Earth?**

◆ Venus

Our next-door neighbor planet is nothing like us! Its surface is hot enough to melt metal, and its atmosphere is thick with poisonous gases.

3 **How long does it take for Earth to make one complete spin?**

◆ One day

Earth spins like a top around an imaginary line called the axis, which runs between the North and South Poles. This complete spin equals our 24-hour day.

4 **Put these life-forms in the order they first appeared on Earth:**

● Bacteria
▲ Fish
◆ Mammals

Single-celled bacteria developed in the ocean about 3.8 billion years ago. Fish came later, then mammals.

5 **300 million years ago, Earth had one giant ocean and a single supercontinent called...**

▲ Pangea

Over millions of years, the rocky plates that make up Earth's surface moved apart, splitting Pangea into the seven continents we know today.

6 Earth's inner core is mostly made of which metal?

▲ Iron

Earth's core of iron is 1,500 miles (2,440 km) wide and its temperature reaches up to 10,832°F (6,000°C)—as hot as the surface of the sun.

7 Earth's crust floats above a layer of hot rock called...

◆ The mantle

Earth's thickest layer is made of superhot, solid rock. Although some parts are liquid rock (magma), which explode from Earth's crust in a volcanic eruption.

8 During which of Earth's geological eras did the dinosaurs first appear?

◆ Mesozoic Era

It lasted for over 185 million years. There was just one giant continent, which dinosaurs roamed across .

9 What causes this natural light show in Earth's polar regions?

⬤ Charged particles from the sun

These glowing lights are called auroras. They occur when solar winds—electrically charged particles from the sun—become trapped by Earth's magnetic field and interact with gases in our atmosphere.

10 What caused the dinosaurs to become extinct—probably?

▲ Asteroid impact

Scientists think an asteroid hit Earth causing a dust cloud to block the sun. Dinosaurs failed to adapt to the new climate.

Podium!

Bronze: 1–5 correct answers
Silver: 6–8 correct answers
Gold: 9–10 correct answers

Fossils

Is your fossil knowledge rock-solid? Time to dig deep in your memory stores and unearth what you know!

1 **True or false: Only the bones of an animal can become a fossil.**
◆ True
▲ False

2 **Which of these are fossils NOT found in?**
◆ Rock
▲ Ice
● Water

3 **"Fossil" comes from the Latin word for...?**
◆ Death
▲ Digging
● History

4 **How often is a fossil of a new dinosaur species discovered?**
◆ Every week
▲ Every year
● Every decade

5 **When was the first complete dinosaur skeleton found?**
◆ 1758
▲ 1858
● 1958

Did you know?
The oldest fossils are 3.5 billion years old! They're stromatolites— mounds of rock made by bacteria in ancient oceans.

6 This fossil of this extinct marine animal has what nickname?

◆ Snakestone
▲ Ropestone
● Snailstone

7 How did seashell fossils end up in the Himalayas, the world's highest mountains?

◆ Ancient sea creatures could climb mountains
▲ They were dropped by prehistoric sea eagles
● The mountains were once part of the seabed

8 What is a fossil trackway?

◆ The remains of an ancient Roman road
▲ Marks left by an animal on the move
● A trench dug by a paleontologist

9 What is the name of this fossilized animal?

◆ Pterodactyl
▲ Trilobite
● Arthropod

10 Which of these body parts is least likely to be fossilized?

◆ Skin
▲ Bones
● Teeth

Turn to page 12 for the answers!

Fossils
Answers

1 True or false: Only the bones of an animal can become a fossil.

▲ False

Plants and any parts of an animal can become fossils. Footprints, eggs, or nests can also be preserved as trace fossils.

2 Which of these are fossils NOT found in?

● Water

Fossils are remains that have been buried in earth, ice, or amber (tree resin) before they can rot away naturally, as most living things do.

3 "Fossil" comes from the Latin word for...?

▲ Digging

The Latin "fosso" means "to dig up." Most fossils are underground and found using tools.

4 How often is a fossil of a new dinosaur species discovered?

◆ Every week

Dinosaurs ruled Earth for 180 million years, so there are plenty of fossils still waiting for paleontologists and amateurs to find.

5 When was the first complete dinosaur skeleton found?

▲ 1858

The Scelidosaurus was a four-legged plant-eater. The 193-million-year-old fossilized skeleton was found by James Harrison in Dorset, UK.

6 This fossil of this extinct animal has what nickname?

◆ Snakestone

These fossils were mistaken for the coiled remains of snakes, but they're actually the shells of Dactylioceras, a type of ammonite.

7 How did seashell fossils end up in the Himalayas, the world's highest mountains?

● The mountains were once part of the seabed

The Himalayas formed when plates under the ocean collided, creating new mountain peaks with fossils in them.

8 What is a fossil trackway?

▲ Marks left by an animal on the move

Trackways, like footprints, tell scientists a lot about the creature that made them, including its weight and length.

9 What is the name of this fossilized animal?

▲ Trilobite

One of the oldest invertebrates (animals without a backbone), trilobites evolved 500 million years ago. These relatives of spiders and crabs scuttled along the ancient ocean floor.

10 Which of these body parts is least likely to be fossilized?

◆ Skin

Bones and teeth are hard so are more likely to stay whole until they become fossils. Studying skin tells us if animals had fur.

Podium!

Bronze: 1–5 correct answers
Silver: 6–8 correct answers
Gold: 9–10 correct answers

Oceans

How deep is your knowledge of our seas and oceans? Dive in and find out!

1 Put the three largest oceans in order, starting with the biggest:
- ◆ Atlantic Ocean
- ▲ Pacific Ocean
- ● Indian Ocean

2 True or false: The oceans contain 50% of all the water on Earth.
- ◆ True
- ▲ False

3 Which of these layers, or zones, of the ocean is the deepest?
- ◆ Sunlight zone
- ▲ Midnight zone
- ● Hadal zone

4 A group of islands, such as Hawaii, is called...
- ◆ A reef
- ▲ An archipelago
- ● A range

5 What is the main force that makes ocean tides flow in and out?
- ◆ Earth's gravity
- ▲ The moon's gravity
- ● The sun's radiation

Did you know?

Only 25 percent of the ocean floor has been explored and charted by humans!

6 Which of these is NOT true?
- ◆ Seas are smaller than oceans
- ▲ Seas contain fresh water
- ● Every sea is joined to an ocean

7 Which of these seas is connected to the Atlantic Ocean?
- ◆ Mediterranean Sea
- ▲ Ross Sea
- ● Red Sea

9 The submersible that reached the deepest part of the ocean in 2012 was called...
- ◆ Undersea Warrior
- ▲ Oceanic Explorer
- ● Deepsea Challenger

8 A scientist who makes maps of the ocean floor is...
- ◆ An aquacologist
- ▲ A paleontologist
- ● An oceanographer

10 The Galapagos Islands are surrounded by which ocean?
- ◆ The Arctic Ocean
- ▲ The Indian Ocean
- ● The Pacific Ocean

Scan the QR code for a Kahoot! about oceans.

Turn to page 16 for the answers!

Oceans
Answers

1 Put the three largest oceans in order, starting with the biggest:

▲ Pacific Ocean
◆ Atlantic Ocean
● Indian Ocean

The Pacific Ocean is bigger than all the others put together—it's also the deepest and the oldest. The smallest oceans are the Southern and Arctic.

2 True or false: The oceans contain 50% of all the water on Earth.

▲ False

In fact, a whopping 97.5 percent of all water is in the oceans, and half of that is in the gigantic Pacific Ocean!

3 Which of these ocean zones is the deepest?

● Hadal zone

In this freezing-cold pitch-black zone, only a few tiny creatures survive on scraps of dead animals that drift down from above.

4 A group of islands, such as Hawaii, is called...

▲ An archipelago

The Hawaii archipelago stretches over 1,500 miles (2,500 km). It was created over 30 million years ago!

5 What is the main force that makes ocean tides flow in and out?

▲ The moon's gravity

As the moon orbits Earth, its gravity tugs at our oceans causing them to rise and fall. This creates our tides.

6
Which of these is NOT true?

▲ Seas contain fresh water

The water in all seas and oceans is saltwater. The fresh water on our planet is stored in rivers, lakes, glaciers, and ice caps.

7
Which of these seas is connected to the Atlantic Ocean?

◆ Mediterranean Sea

The Strait of Gibraltar, between Europe and Africa, connects the two bodies of water.

9
The submersible that reached the deepest part of the ocean in 2012 was called...

● Deepsea Challenger

This little craft, piloted by movie director James Cameron, reached a depth of almost 6.8 miles (11 km) when it hit the Pacific Ocean floor.

8
A scientist who makes maps of the ocean floor is...

● An oceanographer

They often study the oceans on research ships using technology and instruments.

10
The Galapagos Islands are surrounded by which ocean?

● The Pacific Ocean

Marine iguanas have adapted well to the Galapagos islands by living at sea.

Podium!

Bronze: 1–5 correct answers
Silver: 6–8 correct answers
Gold: 9–10 correct answers

Continents

What do you know about the planet's seven biggest chunks of land? Take the quiz and test your continents competence!

1 Put the four biggest continents in order from largest to smallest:
- ◆ Africa
- ▲ Asia
- ● South America
- ■ North America

2 The bald eagle is native to which continent?
- ◆ North America
- ▲ South America
- ● Europe

Did you know?
During the Ice age, North America and Asia were connected by a strip of land called the Bering Land Bridge. Animals and humans both used this natural bridge to migrate to new places.

3 True or false: Most of Asia is in the Northern Hemisphere.
- ◆ True
- ▲ False

4 Which continent has the most countries?
- ◆ Asia
- ▲ Europe
- ● Africa

5 True or false: Every continent but Antarctica has a desert.
◆ True
▲ False

6 Which continent has the world's longest mountain range?
◆ Africa
▲ Asia
● South America

7 Which capital city is in both Europe and Asia?
◆ Beijing, China
▲ Istanbul, Turkey
● Helsinki, Finland

8 On which continent did the first humans live?
◆ North America
▲ Africa
● Asia

9 Which Oceania island is home to these gigantic stone heads?
◆ Easter Island
▲ Christmas Island
● Diwali Island

10 All three of the world's biggest cities are in the continent of...
◆ Europe
▲ North America
● Asia

Scan the QR code for a Kahoot! about continents.

Turn to page 20 for the answers!

Continents

Answers

1 Put the four biggest continents in order from largest to smallest:
- ▲ Asia
- ◆ Africa
- ■ North America
- ● South America

Asia contains many kinds of biome—frozen tundra in the north, parched deserts in the center, and rainforests in the south.

2 The bald eagle is native to which continent?

◆ North America

The magnificent bald eagle, which actually has a head of white feathers, is the national bird of the US.

3 True or false: Most of Asia is in the Northern Hemisphere.

◆ True

Asia stretches down from the Arctic Circle to the equator. It takes up around one-third of all the land on Earth.

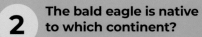

4 Which continent has the most countries?

● Africa

There are 54 African nations recognized by the United Nations, out of a worldwide total of 195 countries.

5 True or false: Every continent but Antarctica has a desert.

▲ False

Every continent on Earth has a desert, including icy Antarctica. Due to its lack of rain, it's classed as a polar desert.

6
Which continent has the world's longest mountain range?

● South America

The Andes mountain range is 4,400 miles (7,000 km) long and stretches down almost the whole continent, through seven countries.

7
Which capital city is in both Europe and Asia?

▲ Istanbul, Turkey

The city is split by water called the Bosphorus Strait. It forms part of the border between Europe and Asia.

8
On which continent did the first humans live?

▲ Africa

The human species *homo sapiens* evolved around 200,000 years ago and, over time, spread across the world.

9
Which Oceania island is home to these gigantic stone heads?

◆ Easter Island

This island is famous for its 887 giant stone heads, called *maoi*. They represent the Islanders' ancient ancestors.

10
All three of the world's biggest cities are in the continent of...

● Asia

They are Tokyo, Japan (40.8 million people); Delhi, India (32.9 million); and Shanghai, China (26.9 million).

Podium!

Bronze: 1–5 correct answers
Silver: 6–8 correct answers
Gold: 9–10 correct answers

Earthquakes

Let's get ready to rumble! Will these quake questions have you shaking your head, or will your answers be faultless?

1 **What causes an earthquake?**
- ◆ Radiation from the sun
- ▲ Changes in Earth's orbit
- ● Movements of Earth's crust

2 **How many earthquakes are there on Earth in a year?**
- ◆ Around 100
- ▲ Around 1,000
- ● Around 20,000

3 **What word describes the exact spot under the ground where an earthquake starts?**
- ◆ Ground zero
- ▲ Center point
- ● Hypocenter

4 **An earthquake spreads out via which type of waves?**
- ◆ Seismic waves
- ▲ Radio waves
- ● Sound waves

Did you know?
The fastest postquake shock waves travel through the ground at up to 17,900 mph (28,800 km/h)!

5 Which of these is used for measuring the strength of earthquakes?

◆ Moment magnitude scale

▲ Beaufort scale

● Scoville scale

6 Which US city was devastated by an earthquake in 1906?

◆ New York

▲ Los Angeles

● San Francisco

7 Which of these events does NOT cause a tsunami?

◆ High tides

▲ Volcanic eruptions

● Earthquakes

8 In 1958, the highest tsunami ever recorded was...

◆ 72 ft (22 m) high

▲ 518 ft (158 m) high

● 1,720 ft (524 m) high

9 Tsunami means "harbor wave" in which language?

◆ Māori

▲ Urdu

● Japanese

10 The strongest land earthquake ever recorded was in which country?

◆ China

▲ Canada

● Chile

Turn to page 24 for the answers!

Earthquakes
Answers

1 **What causes an earthquake?**
● Movements of Earth's crust
Earth's surface is like a huge jigsaw puzzle of plates of rock. When two of these plates shift and collide, the result is a ground-shaking quake!

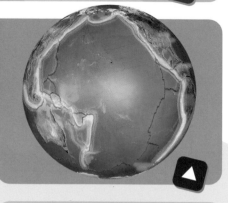

2 **How many earthquakes are there on Earth in a year?**
● Around 20,000
Earthquakes are very common! Most don't cause any damage and are detected only by instruments.

3 **What word describes the exact spot under the ground where an earthquake starts?**
● Hypocenter
A quake begins deep underground at the hypocenter. It sends shock waves to Earth's surface.

4 **An earthquake spreads out via which type of waves?**
◆ Seismic waves
The word comes from the ancient Greek *seismos*, meaning "shock" or "shake." Earthquake tremors are measured using a seismograph.

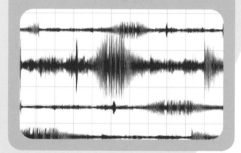

5
Which of these is used for measuring the strength of earthquakes?

◆ Moment magnitude scale

It measures the energy of an earthquake—the higher the number, the greater the power!

6
Which US city was devastated by an earthquake in 1906?

● San Francisco

The 40-second quake caused a fire to engulf the city, destroying up to 30,000 buildings.

7
Which of these events does NOT cause a tsunami?

◆ High tides

Although tsunamis are sometimes called "tidal waves," tides don't cause these wave surges.

8
In 1958, the highest tsunami ever recorded was...

● 1,720 ft (524 m) high

That's higher than New York City's Empire State Building! It hit a remote bay in Alaska.

10
The strongest land earthquake ever recorded was in which country?

● Chile

A 9.5 magnitude quake struck the city of Valdivia in Chile in 1960.

Podium!
Bronze: 1–5 correct answers
Silver: 6–8 correct answers
Gold: 9–10 correct answers

9
Tsunami means "harbor wave" in which language?

● Japanese

Located on the Pacific Ring of Fire, Japan gets more than its fair share of earthquakes and tsunamis.

Rivers

Water travels around the planet in mighty rivers. Just go with the flow and see where these questions take you...

1 Which river runs through Paris, France?
◆ Loire
▲ Seine
● Danube

2 Put the world's three longest rivers in order, with the longest first.
◆ Amazon, South America
▲ Nile, Africa
● Yangtze, Asia

4 In which of these rivers would you find electric eels?
◆ Amazon
▲ Rhine
● Nile

3 Which mighty dam sits on the Colorado River?
◆ Washington Dam
▲ Jefferson Dam
● Hoover Dam

Did you know?
The Amazon River is 4,000 miles (6,400 km) long, but it doesn't have a single bridge! Local people cross the superwide river with boats instead.

5 True or false: The Danube River flows through FOUR European capital cities.

◆ True

▲ False

6 The small grains of rocky material carried by rivers is called...

◆ Sentiment

▲ Sediment

● Supplement

7 The Ganges River in India is sacred to people of which religion?

◆ Buddhism

▲ Hinduism

● Sikhism

8 A smaller river that flows into and joins another, bigger river is called a...

◆ Tributary

▲ Inlet

● Stream

9 What is a river delta?

◆ The place where a river begins

▲ Where a river meets the sea

● A large bend in a river

10 The Thames Barrier in London, UK, was built to:

◆ Prevent flooding

▲ Provide fuel for local homes

● Protect fish from pollution

Scan the QR code for a Kahoot! about rivers.

Turn to page 28 for the answers!

Rivers
Answers

1 **Which river runs through Paris, France?**
▲ Seine
Paris began on a tiny island in the Seine River—the Île de la Cité. The island still has the city's most famous cathedral, Notre-Dame.

2 **Put the world's three longest rivers in order, with the longest first.**
▲ Nile, Africa
◆ Amazon, South America
● Yangtze, Asia
The Nile is 4,160 miles (6,695 km) long and passes through 11 African countries.

3 **Which mighty dam sits on the Colorado River?**
● Hoover Dam
This huge dam is 726 ft (221 m) high. The river water is used to generate power for four US states.

4 **In which of these rivers would you find electric eels?**
◆ Amazon
The electric eels that prowl the Amazon produce four times the voltage of a power point in your home!

5 True or false: The Danube River flows through FOUR European capital cities.

◆ True

The Danube flows through Vienna (Austria), Bratislava (Slovakia), Budapest (Hungary), and Belgrade (Serbia).

8 A smaller river that flows into and joins another, bigger river is called a...

◆ Tributary

Each tributary adds more water to the main river, causing it to swell as it flows toward the sea.

6 The small grains of rocky material carried by rivers is called...

▲ Sediment

When a river floods, it deposits sediment on the land, creating fields called floodplains.

9 What is a river delta?

▲ Where a river meets the sea

As some rivers reach the sea, they deposit sediment creating a delta—a triangular shaped area of land.

10 The Thames Barrier in London, UK, was built to:

◆ Prevent flooding

The barrier was built in 1984 to protect London from floods caused by storm surges.

7 The Ganges River in India is sacred to people of which religion?

▲ Hinduism

Hindu pilgrims gather along the river every 12 years. They believe that bathing in the water will wash away their sins.

Podium!

Bronze: 1–5 correct answers
Silver: 6–8 correct answers
Gold: 9–10 correct answers

Trees

Will these knotty questions about trees leave you stumped? Take the quiz and see if you can log a great score!

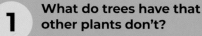

1 What do trees have that other plants don't?
◆ Leaves
▲ Roots
● Trunks

2 The world's oldest tree is...
◆ 180 years old
▲ 1,300 years old
● Nearly 5,000 years old

3 Animals that live in trees are described as...
◆ Marine
▲ Subterranean
● Arboreal

4 The Japanese art of growing tiny trees in trays is called...
◆ Manga
▲ Bonsai
● Origami

Did you know?
Trees communicate with other trees and underground fungi through their roots!

5 In Norse mythology, the giant ash tree that holds up the universe is called...
- ◆ Odin
- ▲ Yggdrasil
- ● Asgard

6 The European Oak tree can be home to how many different species of creatures?
- ◆ 700
- ▲ 1,500
- ● 2,300

7 What species of tree is the tallest on Earth?
- ◆ Coastal redwood
- ▲ Mahogany
- ● Douglas fir

8 What sweet treat is made from the seeds of the cacao tree?
- ◆ Honey
- ▲ Maple syrup
- ● Chocolate

9 Painkilling aspirin pills are made from the bark of which tree?
- ◆ Willow
- ▲ Sycamore
- ● Aspen

Scan the QR code for a Kahoot! about trees.

10 A koala eats leaves from only which tree?
- ◆ Acacia
- ▲ Bottlebrush
- ● Eucalyptus

Turn to page 32 for the answers!

Trees
Answers

1 **What do trees have that other plants don't?**
- Trunks

A tree's trunk makes it a tree! This hard, woody, central stem is strong enough to hold up the tree's branches.

2 **The world's oldest tree is...**
- Nearly 5,000 years old

The bristlecone pine tree is in California. It's older than the pyramids in ancient Egypt by more than 1,000 years!

3 **Animals that live in trees are described as...**
- Arboreal

They often have specially developed claws, tails, or long limbs to help them grip branches or swing from tree to tree.

4 **The Japanese art of growing tiny trees in trays is called...**
- ▲ Bonsai

This ancient skill creates perfect miniature replicas of larger trees. The smallest bonsais are 2 in (5 cm) tall!

5 **In Norse mythology, the giant ash tree that holds up the universe is called...**
- ▲ Yggdrasil

This giant tree house holds all nine worlds of the Norse universe in its branches. Its giant roots are watered by three magical wells.

6 The European Oak tree can be home to how many different species of creatures?

● 2,300

It shelters 30 species of birds and 200 of moths, plus insects, squirrels, mice, and bats.

7 What species of tree is the tallest on Earth?

◆ Coastal redwood

These giants grow in the forests of California. Hyperion is the tallest, at 377 ft (115 m)—the same height as 20 giraffes!

9 Painkilling aspirin pills are made from the bark of which tree?

◆ Willow

Aspirin is widely used as a pain medicine, but willow bark was used to treat fever in ancient Greece 2,000 years ago!

8 What sweet treat is made from the seeds of the cacao tree?

● Chocolate

Seeds (cocoa beans) are sun-dried, shelled, and ground into a paste to make chocolate.

10 A koala eats leaves from only which tree?

● Eucalyptus

The leaves are poisonous, but special bacteria in the koala's gut helps it digest these tough, bitter leaves.

Podium!
Bronze: 1–5 correct answers
Silver: 6–8 correct answers
Gold: 9–10 correct answers

Mountains

Test yourself and your friends with this range of mountain questions and see if you're the cl-Everest!

1 **What is the world's tallest mountain?**
- ◆ K2
- ▲ Mount Everest
- ● Kilimanjaro

2 **Which of these is a way in which mountains are created?**
- ◆ Different plates of Earth's crust collide
- ▲ An asteroid strikes Earth
- ● Strong winds and tides

3 **What's the term for a group of mountains that form a line?**
- ◆ A range
- ▲ A pack
- ● A stretch

4 **On a mountainside, a sudden slide of snow is called...**
- ◆ A glacier
- ▲ An avalanche
- ● A snowflow

Did you know?
Formed 3.6 billion years ago, the Makhonjwa Mountains in South Africa are Earth's oldest peaks!

5 **What is this flat-topped mountain in South Africa called?**
- ◆ Slab Mountain
- ▲ Bald Mountain
- ● Table Mountain

6 Which great apes make their home in Africa's Virunga Mountains?
- ◆ Mountain chimpanzees
- ▲ Mountain orangutans
- ● Mountain gorillas

7 The Matterhorn is in which mountain range?
- ◆ Atlas Mountains
- ▲ Pyrenees
- ● Alps

8 True or false: The Himalayas are Earth's youngest mountain range.
- ◆ True
- ▲ False

9 What is this mountain called?
- ◆ Mount Rushmore
- ▲ Mount Washington
- ● Mount Lincoln

10 Mount Kilimanjaro is the highest point in which continent?
- ◆ Asia
- ▲ Africa
- ● Antarctica

Scan the QR code for a Kahoot! about mountains.

Turn to page 36 for the answers!

Mountains
Answers

1 **What is the world's tallest mountain?**

▲ Mount Everest

It's 29,032 ft (8,849 m) high. The plates below are still pushing together, so it's growing by $4/25$ in (4 mm) each year!

2 **Which of these is a way in which mountains are created?**

◆ Different plates of Earth's crust collide

Mountains formed like this are called fold mountains.

3 **What's the term for a group of mountains that form a line?**

◆ A range

Mountain ranges can be very long! The Andes stretches across almost the whole length of South America, passing through seven countries.

4 **On a mountainside, a sudden slide of snow is called...**

▲ An avalanche

Avalanches can move faster than 199 mph (320 km/h)—they can outrace even the fastest downhill skiers.

5 What is this flat-topped mountain in South Africa called?

● Table Mountain

Its sandstone layers were laid down 500 million years ago. Erosion has worn away the upper layers into the famous table shape.

6 Which great apes make their home in Africa's Virunga Mountains?

● Mountain gorillas

These primates prefer the high life! They live as high up as 1,000 ft (3,000 m).

7 The Matterhorn is in which mountain range?

● Alps

The Matterhorn's pointy peak is called a glacial horn. It was formed by glaciers sliding down the mountainsides.

8 True or false: The Himalayas are Earth's youngest mountain range.

◆ True

At 40 million years old, it's a newcomer in geological terms. It has 10 of the world's highest peaks!

9 What is this US mountain called?

◆ Mount Rushmore

The heads show US Presidents Washington, Jefferson, Roosevelt, and Lincoln.

Podium!

Bronze: 1–5 correct answers

Silver: 6–8 correct answers

Gold: 9–10 correct answers

10 Mount Kilimanjaro is the highest point in which continent?

▲ Africa

Mount Kilimanjaro is an extinct volcano. Its last eruption was 360,000 years ago! The tallest of its three volcanic cones is called Kibo.

Volcanoes

Is your volcano knowledge as red-hot as molten magma? Find out by taking this explosive quiz!

1 The hot, melted rock that erupts from a volcano is called...
◆ Lava
▲ Java
● Magma

2 Someone who studies volcanoes is called a...
◆ Pyrotechnician
▲ Archaeologist
● Volcanologist

3 A volcano that can never erupt again is...
◆ Extinct
▲ Active
● Dormant

Did you know?
The big island of Hawaii is made up of five huge volcanoes, including Kilauea, the world's most active volcano.

4 True or false: There are more active volcanoes below sea than on land.
◆ True
▲ False

5 A huge crater is called a caldera. What does it mean in Spanish?

◆ Fireplace
▲ Cooking pot
● Pimple

6 What type of volcano is Mount Fuji in Japan?

◆ Shield
▲ Cinder cone
● Stratovolcano

7 A fumarole is...

◆ A crack in the ground where hot gas escapes
▲ An undersea spring that spits out hot water
● A fast-flowing cloud of lava and gas

8 When Mount St. Helens erupted in 1980, which warning sign was seen?

◆ The temperature fell
▲ Wildlife fled the area
● A bulge in the mountainside

9 Where is the largest volcano in the solar system?

◆ Mars
▲ Venus
● The moon

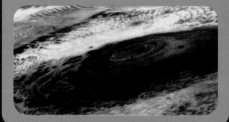

Scan the QR code for a Kahoot! about volcanoes.

10 Where is Earth's largest volcanic region?

◆ North America
▲ Europe
● Antarctica

Turn to page 40 for the answers!

Volcanoes
Answers

1 **The hot, melted rock that erupts from a volcano is called...**

◆ Lava

When the hot, liquid rock called magma flows onto Earth's surface, it gets a new name—lava!

2 **Someone who studies volcanoes is called a...**

● Volcanologist

This protective suit has a metal coating that reflects the heat of the volcano, leaving the person cool inside. The suit can withstand temperatures of 3,000°F (1650°C)!

3 **A volcano that can never erupt again is...**

◆ Extinct

The UK's highest mountain, Ben Nevis, has been extinct for 350 million years!

4 **True or false: There are more active volcanoes below sea than on land.**

◆ True

So far, scientists have found around a million underwater volcanoes.

5 A huge crater is called a caldera. What does it mean in Spanish?

▲ Cooking pot

Often, these massive craters fill with water to form a lake.

6 What type of volcano is Mount Fuji in Japan?

● Stratovolcano

Fuji's cone shape is formed by layers of lava and ash from past eruptions.

8 When Mount St. Helens erupted in 1980, which warning sign was seen?

● A bulge in the mountainside

Before the eruption, the bulge grew bigger by 3 feet (1 m) a day.

7 A fumarole is...

◆ A crack in the ground where hot gas escapes

The sulfur-filled gas jets smell strongly of rotten eggs. Eew!

9 Where is the largest volcano in the solar system?

◆ Mars

Olympus Mons is 5 miles (8 km) high—that's twice as high as Earth's Mount Everest.

Podium!

Bronze: 1–5 correct answers
Silver: 6–8 correct answers
Gold: 9–10 correct answers

10 Where is Earth's largest volcanic region?

● Antarctica

There are more than 130 volcanoes under the ice in West Antarctica.

Hot Springs and Geysers

Sometimes Earth preheats its water, creating springs or geysers. Let's see if you're hot stuff when it comes to hot springs!

1 What's the scientific term for hot springs and geysers?
- ◆ Thermonuclear features
- ▲ Geothermal features
- ● Hydrostatic features

2 Which substance is the source of the heat that creates geothermal features?
- ◆ Magma
- ▲ Steam
- ● Coal

3 Which US National Park contains half of all the planet's geothermal features?
- ◆ Yellowstone
- ▲ Yosemite
- ● Great Smoky Mountains

4 This is Pamukkale hot spring in Turkey. What does it mean in Turkish?
- ◆ Cotton castle
- ▲ Snow terrace
- ● White shelves

5 Which geyser has the world's highest jet of water?
- ◆ Old Faithful
- ▲ Steamboat
- ● Porkchop

6 What causes the spectacular colors in some hot springs?
◆ Pools of oil
▲ Microbes
● Underwater flowers

7 A hot spring that occurs under the sea is called a...
◆ Blue geyser
▲ Green steamer
● Black smoker

9 In which country would you find these macaques taking a warm bath?
◆ Greenland
▲ Japan
● Norway

8 Pools of boiling, sludgy soil are called...
◆ Sludge ponds
▲ Mud springs
● Mud pots

10 In which country are 90 percent of homes linked to a geothermal heating system?
◆ Scotland
▲ Iceland
● Russia

Did you know?

Iceland has its very own boiling river! The Deildartunguhver hot springs send out 65 gallons (245 liters) of water every second.

Turn to page 44 for the answers!

Hot Springs and Geysers
Answers

1 What's the scientific term for hot springs and geysers?

▲ Geothermal features

Geysers are high-pressure jets of water. Hot springs are pools that are fed by a constant water supply.

2 Which substance is the source of the heat that creates geothermal features?

◆ Magma

This red-hot, liquid rock rises near Earth's surface. It heats up the water in or on the ground.

4 This is Pamukkale hot spring in Turkey. What does it mean in Turkish?

◆ Cotton castle

White terraces have been created by the limestone in the water as it flows down the mountain.

3 Which US National Park contains half of all the planet's geothermal features?

◆ Yellowstone

A supervolcano under the park creates all that hot-water action!

5 Which geyser has the world's highest jet of water?

▲ Steamboat

All three geysers are in Yellowstone. Steamboat shoots water more than 300 ft (90 m) high.

6
What causes the spectacular colors in some hot springs?

▲ Microbes

These tiny, colorful microorganisms, called archaea, thrive in high temperatures where very few other living things can survive.

7
A hot spring that occurs under the sea is called a...

● Black smoker

These chimney-shaped ocean hot spots are also known as hydrothermal vents. Its hot water is rich in minerals.

8
Pools of boiling, sludgy soil are called...

● Mud pots

Magma releases chemicals that melt rocks. The boiling gloop bubbles to the surface, creating mud pots.

9
In which country would you find these macaques taking a warm bath?

▲ Japan

These macaques live in Japan's snow-covered mountains and forests. They're also known as snow monkeys!

10
In which country are 90 percent of homes linked to a geothermal heating system?

▲ Iceland

Heat from volcanoes produces most of Iceland's electricity and hot water.

Podium!
Bronze: 1–5 correct answers
Silver: 6–8 correct answers
Gold: 9–10 correct answers

Caves

Explore the darkest depths of your memory and see if you can figure out the answers to these cool cave questions.

1 True or false: Most caves are formed by the action of rainwater.
- ◆ True
- ▲ False

2 In 2018, a team of young soccer players was rescued from flooded caves in which country?
- ◆ US
- ▲ Italy
- ● Thailand

3 What is the scientific study of caves?
- ◆ Profundology
- ▲ Cavology
- ● Speleology

4 Fingers of rock that hang from a cave's ceiling are called...
- ◆ Stalagmites
- ▲ Stalactites
- ● Cave columns

5 Roughly how long ago did Aboriginal artists paint this image?

◆ 80,000 years ago
▲ 40,000 years ago
● 25,000 years ago

6 How deep is the deepest cave ever discovered?

◆ 1,640 ft (500 m)
▲ 0.7 miles (1.1 km)
● 1.4 miles (2.2 km)

7 A cave made from the flow of molten volcanic rock is called a...

◆ Magma tunnel
▲ Lava tube
● Eruption cavern

8 Animals that are adapted to spend their whole lives in dark caves are called...

◆ Troglobites
▲ Photobites
● Vampirabites

9 Which of these is the world's longest system of caves?

◆ Elephant Cave, Scotland
▲ Mammoth Cave, US
● Blue Whale Cave, Canada

Did you know?
The longest stalactite ever found is 92 ft (28 m) long—the height of five giraffes!

10 How many bats live in Bracken Cave in Texas, US?

◆ 100,000
▲ 1 million
● 20 million

Turn to page 48 for the answers!

Caves
Answers

1 True or false: Most caves are formed by the action of rainwater.

◆ True

Most caves form over thousands of years as rainwater seeps through underground rock and slowly erodes it.

2 In 2018, a team of young soccer players was rescued from flooded caves in which country?

● Thailand

The boys were trapped for nine days. The rescue team included divers from many countries, including Australia and the UK.

3 What is the scientific study of caves?

● Speleology

Speleologists study all aspects of caves: how they are formed and what they're made of. The word comes from the ancient Greek for cave!

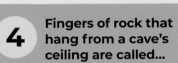

4 Fingers of rock that hang from a cave's ceiling are called...

▲ Stalactites

Water dripping through the cave ceiling carries limestone, which forms dangling shapes called stalactites.

5 Roughly how long ago did Aboriginal artists paint this image?

▲ 40,000 years ago

This rock art, in Ubirr Australia, shows an image of a turtle and provides a record of Aboriginal life.

6 How deep is the deepest cave ever discovered?

● 1.4 miles (2.2 km)

The Veryovkina Cave was discovered in 2018, in Georgia, on the border between Europe and Asia. Scientists believe deeper caves exist!

7 A cave made from the flow of molten volcanic rock is called a...

▲ Lava tube

These caves were filled with hot lava flowing inside a hard outer crust of cooled lava. Now they are rocky tunnels!

8 Animals that are adapted to spend their whole lives in dark caves are called...

◆ Troglobites

They have no eyes or poorly developed eyes. Eyes aren't needed in the dark!

9 Which of these is the world's longest system of caves?

▲ Mammoth Cave, US

This system stretches more than 400 miles (644 km). It contains rivers, rock formations, fossils, and drawings.

10 How many bats live in Bracken Cave in Texas, US?

● 20 million

20 million Mexican free-tailed bats live in this 100 ft (30 m) wide cave. It's the world's biggest colony of bats.

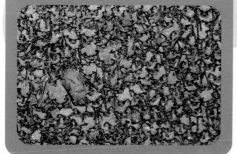

Podium!

Bronze: 1–5 correct answers
Silver: 6–8 correct answers
Gold: 9–10 correct answers

Rocks, Minerals, and Gems

Time to hit the hard stuff and find out if your geology knowledge is rock solid... or a little rocky?

1 A rock is a solid clump of...
- ◆ Gases
- ▲ Liquids
- ● Minerals

2 The oldest rocks we know about on Earth are more than...
- ◆ 20 million years old
- ▲ 4.2 billion years old
- ● 20.5 billion years old

Did you know?

The most expensive gemstone ever is a diamond called CTF Pink Star. It sold in 2017 for an eye-watering $71.2 million (£56.8 million)!

3 What is erosion?
- ◆ When rocks break down or wear away
- ▲ When rocks melt in a volcanic eruption
- ● When rocks freeze inside a glacier

4 What are diamonds made of?
- ◆ Ice
- ▲ Glass
- ● Carbon

5 The scientific study of Earth's rocks and minerals is called...
- ◆ Archaeology
- ▲ Geology
- ● Cosmology

6 This rock is Uluru in Australia. What is it made of?

◆ Granite
▲ Limestone
● Sandstone

7 True or false: The gemstones sapphire and ruby both come from the same mineral.

◆ True
▲ False

8 How does igneous rock form?

◆ When fragments of asteroids fall to Earth
▲ When melted magma cools and hardens
● When layers of fossils build up and stick together

9 The biggest diamond ever found was discovered in...

◆ South Africa
▲ India
● Antarctica

10 Which famous rock formation was created by rapidly cooled lava?

◆ Grand Canyon, US
▲ Giant's Causeway, UK
● Wadi Rum, Jordan

Scan the QR code for a Kahoot! about rocks, minerals, and gems.

Turn to page 52 for the answers!

Rocks, Minerals, and Gems

Answers

1 **A rock is a solid clump of...**
● Minerals
A mineral is a natural, solid substance. It's found in gemstones, toothpaste—and even our bones!

2 **The oldest rocks we know about on Earth are more than...**
▲ 4.2 billion years old
The oldest known rocks are a type called gneiss found in Eastern Canada. It's a metamorphic rock, formed by super-intense heat or pressure.

3 **What is erosion?**
◆ When rocks break down or wear away
Rocks can be eroded by rain, rivers, or a glacier. In deserts, winds can sculpt rocks into odd shapes, as this photo shows!

4 **What are diamonds made of?**
● Carbon
Carbon is a versatile element. It also forms coal, oil, graphite (the "lead" in pencils), and all the life on Earth.

5 The scientific study of Earth's rocks and minerals is called...

▲ Geology

Geologists study all aspects of rocks—the minerals that form them and how they've shaped our Earth.

6 This rock is Uluru in Australia. What is it made of?

● Sandstone

As sedimentary rock, it was made by sand layers being pressed together over millions of years.

7 True or false: The gemstones sapphire and ruby both come from the same mineral.

◆ True

Both gems are varieties of corundum—Earth's second-hardest mineral. Generally, rubies are red and sapphires are blue.

8 How does igneous rock form?

▲ When melted magma cools and hardens

Igneous rock is the leftover evidence of our planet's volcanic and violent past.

9 The biggest diamond ever found was discovered in...

◆ South Africa

The Cullinan diamond was 4 in (10 cm) long and 2½ in (6.4 cm) wide—the size of a big fist!

10 Which famous rock formation was created by rapidly cooled lava?

▲ Giant's Causeway, UK

60 million years ago, a volcano spewed molten basalt. As it cooled, 40,000 hexagonal columns formed!

Podium!

Bronze: 1–5 correct answers

Silver: 6–8 correct answers

Gold: 9–10 correct answers

Lakes

Plunge into these water-themed puzzlers and find out whether your knowledge is deeper than a lake or as shallow as a pond!

1 **What's the world's deepest lake?**
- ◆ Lake Baikal, Russia
- ▲ Lake Tanganyika, East Africa
- ● Crater Lake, US

2 **Which of these is NOT one of North America's Great Lakes?**
- ◆ Huron
- ▲ Ontario
- ● Victoria

3 **These birds at Lake Nakuru, Kenya, are called...**
- ◆ Flamingos
- ▲ Storks
- ● Pelicans

Did you know?

Finland's nickname "The Land of a Thousand Lakes" is seriously inaccurate. There are actually more than 187,000 lakes in the country!

5 **What's unusual about Lake Vostok?**
- ◆ Its water is reddish in color.
- ▲ It was formed by an asteroid strike.
- ● It lies under 2.5 miles (4 km) of ice.

4 **Which "sea" is really a lake?**
- ◆ Caspian Sea
- ▲ Red Sea
- ● Storm Sea

6 The study of lakes is called...
◆ Hydrology
▲ Limnology
● Lakeology

7 In which country are these floating homes?
◆ Japan
▲ Peru
● Ireland

8 True or false: Great Salt Lake, Utah, is more salty than the sea.
◆ True
▲ False

9 Crater Lake in Oregon was formed by...
◆ A melted glacier
▲ A meteorite strike
● A collapsed volcano crater

Scan the QR code for a Kahoot! about lakes.

10 In which European country is Lake Garda?
◆ Spain
▲ The UK
● Italy

Turn to page 56 for the answers!

Lakes
Answers

1 **What's the world's deepest lake?**

◆ Lake Baikal, Russia

It's at least 5.6 miles (9 km) deep and contains one-fifth of the world's fresh water!

2 **Which of these is NOT one of North America's Great Lakes?**

● Victoria

Victoria is one of Africa's lakes. North America's Great Lakes are Superior, Ontario, Huron, Michigan, and Erie.

3 **These birds at Lake Nakuru, Kenya, are called...**

◆ Flamingos

These beautiful birds gather at Lake Nakuru and neighboring Lake Bogoria, in East Africa, to feed on algae (water plants).

4 **Which "sea" is really a lake?**

◆ Caspian Sea

Although it's larger than many seas, the Caspian Sea, between Europe and Asia, is surrounded by land, so that makes it a lake—the biggest in the world!

5 **What's unusual about Lake Vostok?**

● It lies under 2.5 miles (4 km) of ice.

Antarctica's vast ice sheet covers more than 360 lakes! Lake Vostok is the largest known subglacial lake.

6. The study of lakes is called...

▲ Limnology

Limnologists study all inland waters, including rivers, wetlands, and ponds, as well as human-made lakes called reservoirs.

7. In which country are these floating homes?

▲ Peru

Titicaca is one of the world's highest lakes at 2.5 miles (4 km) above sea level. More than 40 floating islands are on the lake, built by the Uros people from reeds that grow by the lake.

9. Crater Lake in Oregon was formed by...

● A collapsed volcano crater

More than 7,000 years ago, a volcano erupted and collapsed, leaving a huge crater that filled with water. It's the US's deepest lake.

8. True or false: Great Salt Lake, Utah, is more salty than the sea.

◆ True

It's five times saltier than seawater! Great Salt Lake is a closed water basin, so the water escapes only by evaporation. When the water evaporates, it leaves areas of salty minerals, called salt flats.

10. In which European country is Lake Garda?

● Italy

Lake Garda is Italy's largest lake. Like many lakes in the region, it was formed in the Ice Age by a glacier that slid to the base of a mountain and melted.

Podium!

Bronze: 1–5 correct answers
Silver: 6–8 correct answers
Gold: 9–10 correct answers

Ice

Chill out with these cool questions all about ice and the incredible array of frozen formations it creates.

1 Which continent is almost entirely covered in ice?
- ◆ Asia
- ▲ Oceania
- ● Antarctica

Did you know?
Global warming means that Earth's ice is now melting at a rate of 1.2 trillion tons (1 trillion metric tons) per year.

2 A gigantic mass of ice that moves slowly over land is...
- ◆ A glacier
- ▲ An icefall
- ● An ice river

3 True or false: Icebergs are made of frozen seawater.
- ◆ True
- ▲ False

4 Which word describes ice breaking off a glacier to become an iceberg?
- ◆ Birthing
- ▲ Harvesting
- ● Calving

5 What doggy term is used for the smaller chunks of ice that break off icebergs?
- ◆ Growler
- ▲ Barker
- ● Rover

6 Vast areas of the world are covered in frozen soil that never thaws. What is this called?

◆ Ice cap
▲ Permafrost
● Ice floe

7 At its thickest, about how deep is the ice over Antarctica?

◆ 330 ft (100 m)
▲ 1.25 miles (2 km)
● 3 miles (5 km)

8 True or false: The world's fastest-moving glacier moves quicker than a polar bear.

◆ True
▲ False

9 What is this free-floating ice called?

◆ Island ice
▲ Pack ice
● Pancake ice

10 In 1912, which famous ship hit an iceberg and sank on its first voyage?

◆ *Queen Mary*
▲ *Titanic*
● *Lusitania*

Turn to page 60 for the answers!

Ice

Answers

1 Which continent is almost entirely covered in ice?

● Antarctica

The huge ice sheet that covers Antarctica contains about 90 percent of all the ice in the world!

2 A gigantic mass of ice that moves slowly over land is...

◆ A glacier

Most glaciers develop in the mountains, where fallen snow piles up over hundreds of years and presses down to form a solid block.

3 True or false: Icebergs are made of frozen seawater.

▲ False

An iceberg is a chunk of frozen fresh water that breaks away from an ice cap or glacier on the land and floats off into the sea.

4 Which word describes ice breaking off a glacier to become an iceberg?

● Calving

Cracks appear and, over time, a block of ice, up to 200 ft (60 m), crashes into the sea.

5 What doggy term is used for the smaller chunks of ice that break off icebergs?

◆ Growler

The smallest growlers are hard to spot in the water and can be a hazard to passing ships.

6 Vast areas of the world are covered in frozen soil that never thaws. What is this called?

▲ Permafrost

In North Siberia, Russia, the hard permafrost, which lies under the top soil layer, is 0.9 miles (1,500 m) thick!

8 True or false: The world's fastest-moving glacier moves quicker than a polar bear.

▲ False

Greenland's Jakobshavn Glacier moves at 130 ft (40 m) per day. That's speedy for a glacier, but polar bears can run at 35 mph (56 km/h)!

7 At its thickest, about how deep is the ice over Antarctica?

● Around 3 miles (5 km)

The Antarctic ice sheet contains nearly 70 percent of all the world's fresh water.

9 What is this free-floating ice called?

▲ Pack ice

In the Arctic Ocean, these mini-islands provide a welcome resting place for seabirds, seals, and polar bears.

10 In 1912, which famous ship hit an iceberg and sank on its first voyage?

▲ *Titanic*

It sank off Newfoundland, Canada, in "Iceberg Alley"—named for the large number of icebergs in that part of the Atlantic Ocean. 1,500 people lost their lives.

Podium!

Bronze: 1–5 correct answers

Silver: 6–8 correct answers

Gold: 9–10 correct answers

Ocean Floor

Dredge the depths of your mind to see what you know about the dark, cold world at the bottom of the ocean.

1 How much of Earth's surface is covered by the ocean?
- ◆ 10%
- ▲ 50%
- ● 70%

2 True or false: The ocean floor is mostly flat.
- ◆ True
- ▲ False

Did you know?

"Marine snow" is the tiny remains of dead fish that drift down from the sunlight zone. It's a lifeline for animals on the dark ocean floor where food is scarce.

3 The scientific study of ocean floor features is...
- ◆ Aquametry
- ▲ Bathymetry
- ● Marimetry

4 Which marine mammal dives the deepest?
- ◆ Seal
- ▲ Whale
- ● Dolphin

5 True or false: The giant barrel sea sponge is a type of plant.
◆ True
▲ False

6 The world's deepest shipwreck is...
◆ *RMS Titanic*
▲ *USS Samuel B. Roberts*
● *Mary Rose*

7 True or false: The water at the ocean floor can reach a sizzling 752°F (400°C).
◆ True
▲ False

8 The first ocean floor cable between Europe and North America was laid in...
◆ 1858
▲ 1958
● 2001

9 According to Greek philosopher Plato, which island sank to the ocean floor after a tsunami?
◆ Artemis
▲ Atlantis
● Acropolis

10 The deepest point in the ocean is...
◆ Enterprise Deep
▲ Discovery Deep
● Challenger Deep

Turn to page 64 for the answers!

Ocean Floor Answers

1 How much of Earth's surface is covered by the ocean?

● 70%

Almost three-quarters of Earth lies underwater. Only a small area is mapped, so there's still lots to explore!

2 True or false: The ocean floor is mostly flat.

◆ True

More than 70 percent of the ocean floor is a flatland called the Abyssal Plain. (There are mountains and trenches, too!)

3 The scientific study of ocean floor features is...

▲ Bathymetry

The word is made up of two Greek words: *bathys*, meaning "depth," and *metron*, meaning "measure."

4 Which marine mammal dives the deepest?

▲ Whale

The Cuvier's beaked whale (pictured) has reached depths of nearly 1.9 miles (3 km). It eats creatures, such as squid, from the ocean floor.

5 True or false: The giant barrel sea sponge is a type of plant.

▲ False

Sponges are animals that sit on the ocean floor. They feed by soaking up seawater through their body.

6 The world's deepest shipwreck is...?

▲ *USS Samuel B. Roberts*

This US Navy ship sank during World War II. It lies 4.2 miles (6.8 km) deep, at the bottom of the Philippine Sea.

7 True or false: The water at the ocean floor can reach a sizzling 752°F (400°C).

◆ True

This occurs at hydrothermal vents (black smokers). Earth's crust spurts out water heated by undersea volcanoes.

8 The first ocean floor cable between Europe and North America was laid in...

◆ 1858

The cable was laid by the *SS Great Eastern* ship. Messages were sent using a telegraph system and took 17 minutes to cross the ocean!

9 According to Greek philosopher Plato, which island sank to the ocean floor after a tsunami?

▲ Atlantis

There's no scientific evidence that Plato's paradise island really existed, but divers and marine archaeologists continue to look for it, just in case!

10 The deepest point in the ocean is...

● Challenger Deep

At 6.8 miles (10.9 km) under the surface, it's deep! It would take 29 Empire State Buildings stacked end to end to reach it.

Podium!
Bronze: 1–5 correct answers
Silver: 6–8 correct answers
Gold: 9–10 correct answers

Clouds

Soft and fluffy, gray and gloomy—it's time to find out how informed you are about the different clouds that float above us.

1 **What are clouds made of?**
- ◆ Water and air
- ▲ Hydrogen and oxygen
- ● Mist and fog

2 **Which of these is NOT a type of cloud?**
- ◆ Stratus
- ▲ Cumulus
- ● Diplodocus

Did you know?

A cumulus cloud can weigh between 550–1,100 tons—as much as four passenger jet planes!

3 **Clouds release rain when...**
- ◆ The temperature rises above 68°F (20°C).
- ▲ Their water droplets get too heavy to hang in the air.
- ● Strong winds blow them apart.

4 **Cirrus clouds get their name from the Latin word for...**
- ◆ Sheet
- ▲ Curl
- ● Dog

5 These UFO-like clouds are called...?
◆ Pancake clouds
▲ Lenticular clouds
● Flying saucer clouds

6 True or false: Fog is a type of cloud.
◆ True
▲ False

7 What is the highest cloud type of all?
◆ Altostratus
▲ Noctilucent
● Cirrus

8 Why does the great frigate bird fly into clouds on purpose?
◆ To ride warm air currents
▲ To drink water droplets
● To hide from predators

Scan the QR code for a Kahoot! about clouds.

9 Which cloud type often causes thunderstorms?
◆ Cumulonimbus
▲ Cirrostratus
● Stratocumulus

Turn to page 68 for the answers!

Clouds
Answers

1 **What are clouds made of?**

◆ Water and air

A cloud is a collection of very tiny water droplets suspended in the air. In higher clouds, the water droplets freeze and become ice.

2 **Which of these is NOT a type of cloud?**

● Diplodocus

Diplodocus was a huge dinosaur! Stratus clouds look like a thin sheet. Cumulus clouds are tall and fluffy.

3 **Clouds release rain when...**

▲ Their water droplets get too heavy to hang in the air.

Inside the cloud, tiny droplets merge to make bigger and bigger ones. When the air can no longer hold the droplets, the rain begins!

4 **Cirrus clouds get their name from the Latin word for...**

▲ Curl

These feathery, wispy clouds form at high altitudes and often hold ice crystals rather than water.

5 **These UFO-like clouds are called...**

▲ Lenticular clouds

Lenticular (lens-shaped) clouds form near mountain ranges. Like UFOs, they can hover for hours!

6 **True or false: Fog is a type of cloud.**

◆ True

Fog is simply a cloud that sits near the ground instead of floating in the air.

7 **What is the highest cloud type of all?**

▲ Noctilucent

Noctilucent (night-shining) clouds form at altitudes of up to 53 miles (85 km). They're visible only at twilight.

8 **Why does the great frigate bird fly into clouds on purpose?**

◆ To ride warm air currents

The strong upward currents inside clouds can keep this seabird airborne for days, or even months, with only an occasional flap of its wings!

9 **Which cloud type often causes thunderstorms?**

◆ Cumulonimbus

These massive, menacing clouds are tall and dark, with flat, wide tops. They are formed by strong updrafts of warm, moist air.

Podium!
Bronze: 1–5 correct answers
Silver: 6–8 correct answers
Gold: 9–10 correct answers

Extreme Weather

These questions on the world's weirdest, wildest weather will go down a storm with you and your friends!

1 **Which of these is NOT a type of lightning?**
- ◆ Ball lightning
- ▲ Forked lightning
- ● Slash lightning

2 **What's another word we use for a tornado?**
- ◆ Wheeler
- ▲ Twister
- ● Hoofer

3 **Where do hurricanes form?**
- ◆ Over the ocean
- ▲ Over mountains
- ● Underground

4 **Why does the sound of thunder happen after a lightning flash?**
- ◆ Sound travels more slowly than light
- ▲ The sound comes from farther away
- ● The sound bounces off the clouds

5 In the US, the area where most tornadoes happen is known as...
◆ Tornado Highway
▲ Tornado Alley
● Tornado Corridor

6 The very center of a hurricane is called the...
◆ Eye
▲ Heart
● Navel

7 Where is the wettest place in the world?
◆ Manchester, UK
▲ Mawsynram, India
● Manila, Philippines

8 What's the Arabic word for a Saharan sandstorm?
◆ Hamam
▲ Hummus
● Haboob

10 The largest hailstones can be as big as...
◆ A golf ball
▲ A tennis ball
● A soccer ball

9 True or false: The world's coldest city is in Iceland.
◆ True
▲ False

Scan the QR code for a Kahoot! about extreme weather.

Did you know?
The highest recorded temperature is a sizzling 134°F (56.7°C). It was recorded in 1913 in the aptly named Furnace Creek, California!

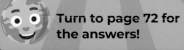 Turn to page 72 for the answers!

Extreme Weather

Answers

1 **Which of these is NOT a type of lightning?**

● Slash lightning

Forked lightning divides into branches—like a fork! Ball lightning is a luminous white sphere shape, and it's very rare!

2 **What's another word we use for a tornado?**

▲ Twister

These swirling columns form in humid weather and hang from thunder clouds. It destroys everything in its path.

3 **Where do hurricanes form?**

◆ Over the ocean

A hurricane starts as a huge thunderstorm over warm waters, gathering strength as it moves over the ocean.

4 **Why does the sound of thunder happen after a lightning flash?**

◆ Sound travels more slowly than light

Thunder and lightning happen together, but light travels faster than sound, so we see the lightning first.

5 In the US, the area where most tornadoes happen is known as...

▲ Tornado Alley

Most of the world's destructive tornadoes happen along the US's Midwest strip.

6 The very center of a hurricane is called the...

◆ Eye

A hurricane's eye is calm, but it's surrounded by strong winds reaching 160 mph (260 km/h)!

7 Where is the wettest place in the world?

▲ Mawsynram, India

This village gets around 467 in (11,872 mm) of rain a year. In June 2022, more than 3 feet (1 m) of rain fell in 24 hours!

8 What's the Arabic word for a Saharan sandstorm?

● Haboob

These walls of sand or dust can be 15 miles (24 km) long and travel at 35 mph (56 km/h)!

9 True or false: The world's coldest city is in Iceland.

▲ False

It's in Yakutsk in Siberia, Russia. Temperatures are often –34.6°F (–37°C) and can get colder!

10 The largest hailstones can be as big as...

● A soccer ball

Most hailstones are pea-size, but the largest recorded hailstone, in South Dakota, weighed 2 lb 3 oz (1 kg)! Luckily, it didn't land on anyone's head!

Podium!
Bronze: 1–5 correct answers
Silver: 6–8 correct answers
Gold: 9–10 correct answers

Rainforests

They're leafy and bursting with spectacular animals. What do you know about Earth's awesome rainforests?

1 The largest rainforest in the world is in...
- ◆ Asia
- ▲ Africa
- ● South America

2 True or false: Most rainforest trees are evergreen.
- ◆ True
- ▲ False

3 What type of bird is the scarlet macaw?
- ◆ Parrot
- ▲ Eagle
- ● Crow

4 What's the difference between temperate and tropical rainforests?
- ◆ Tropical rainforests get more rain
- ▲ Tropical rainforests are larger
- ● Tropical rainforests are hotter

5 Put these layers of a rainforest in order of their height, starting with the lowest.
- ◆ Canopy
- ▲ Forest floor
- ● Emergent layer
- ■ Understory

Did you know?

About a quarter of the ingredients for human medicines comes from rainforest plants!

6 Can you identify this rainforest snake?
- ◆ Emerald tree boa
- ▲ Green mamba
- ● Tree viper

7 Which important gas do rainforest trees release into the atmosphere?
- ◆ Methane
- ▲ Oxygen
- ● Nitrogen

8 What is the name for a rainforest plant that grows on a tree?
- ◆ Epilogue
- ▲ Epiphyte
- ● Epidemic

9 Which Amazon rainforest animal is this?
- ◆ Marmoset
- ▲ Pangolin
- ● Sloth

10 Which is the only continent with no rainforests?
- ◆ Europe
- ▲ Asia
- ● Antarctica

Scan the QR code for a Kahoot! about rainforests.

 Turn to page 76 for the answers!

Rainforests
Answers

1 The largest rainforest in the world is in...

● South America

The vast Amazon Rainforest stretches across nine South American countries and is about the same size as Australia!

2 True or false: Most rainforest trees are evergreen.

◆ True

Evergreen trees keep their leaves all year round. They don't need to drop their leaves to save energy.

3 What type of bird is the scarlet macaw?

◆ Parrot

These chatty birds can live almost as long as humans. They eat nuts and seeds.

4 What's the difference between temperate and tropical rainforests?

● Tropical rainforests are hotter

Tropical rainforests are close to Earth's equator. Temperate rainforests are farther away, where it's cooler.

5 Put these layers of a rainforest in order of their height, starting with the lowest.

▲ Forest floor

■ Understory

◆ Canopy

● Emergent layer

Each layer is a home for different plant species and animals, depending on how much sunshine they need.

76

6 Can you identify this rainforest snake?

◆ Emerald tree boa

This crafty crusher kills its prey by tightly squeezing its coils around a mammal or bird. Then it swallows it whole!

7 Which important gas do rainforest trees release into the atmosphere?

▲ Oxygen

One leafy rainforest tree releases enough oxygen in its growing season for 10 people to breathe for a year!

8 What is the name for a rainforest plant that grows on a tree?

▲ Epiphyte

There's not much light on the ground, so epiphytes grow high up in the trees to catch the sun.

9 Which Amazon rainforest animal is this?

● Sloth

Sloths use their very long, curved claws to hang upside down from branches. They don't move much, and when they do, they are very, very slow!

10 Which is the only continent with no rainforests?

● Antarctica

There are no trees of any kind in Antarctica— it's way too cold, and there isn't enough liquid water for them to survive.

Podium!

Bronze: 1–5 correct answers

Silver: 6–8 correct answers

Gold: 9–10 correct answers

Deserts

If you're thirsty for fun facts about Earth's driest places, try this dastardly desert quiz!

1 What is the world's largest hot desert?
- ◆ Atacama
- ▲ Kalahari
- ● Sahara

2 The definition of a desert is a place that has...
- ◆ Less than 1 in (25 mm) of rain a year
- ▲ A temperature of 95°F (35°C)
- ● Less than 10 in (250 mm) of rain a year

3 What is this desert resident called?
- ◆ Arabian oryx
- ▲ African antelope
- ● Gobi gazelle

4 The driest desert in the world is...
- ◆ Negev
- ▲ Antarctica
- ● Atacama

5 What type of desert plant is this Joshua tree?
- ◆ Cactus
- ▲ Yucca
- ● Palm tree

6 The Atlantic shore of the Namib Desert in Africa is called...
◆ The Forgotten Coast
▲ The Hidden Coast
● The Skeleton Coast

7 Which Australian desert is named after a British Queen?
◆ The Great Victorian Desert
▲ The Queen Camilla Desert
● The Elizabeth Desert

8 True or false: A saguaro cactus can live for 200 years.
◆ True
▲ False

9 The Gobi Desert stretches over which two countries?
◆ Russia and China
▲ China and Mongolia
● India and Pakistan

Did you know?
In some parts of Antarctica, it hasn't rained for 14 million years!

10 Many desert animals are nocturnal. This means they...
◆ Eat insects
▲ Lay eggs
● Are most active at night

Scan the QR code for a Kahoot! about deserts.

Turn to page 80 for the answers!

Deserts Answers

1 **What is the world's largest hot desert?**
● Sahara
With towering dunes and endless seas of sand, the Sahara Desert covers most of North Africa and spreads across 11 countries.

2 **The definition of a desert is a place that has...**
● Less than 10 in (250 mm) of rain a year
Deserts can be hot or cold, and the ground can be sandy, rocky, or icy. But a desert must be very, very dry!

4 **The driest desert in the world is...**
● Atacama
Some areas in Chile's Atacama Desert, in the shadow of the Andes mountains, have never recorded a drop of rain!

3 **What is this desert resident called?**
◆ Arabian oryx
These long-horned antelopes can go weeks without a drink. They get the water they need from munching on desert plants.

5 **What type of desert plant is this Joshua tree?**
▲ Yucca
This spiky-leaved plant grows only in the Mojave Desert in North America. It provides essential food and shelter for many desert animals.

6 The Atlantic shore of the Namib Desert in Africa is called...

● The Skeleton Coast

This bleak, foggy strip gets its spooky name from the shipwrecks and animal bones that have washed up on its shores.

7 Which Australian desert is named after a British Queen?

◆ The Great Victorian Desert

The largest desert in Australia is home to more than 100 different species of reptiles, as well as mammals such as dingos and endangered marsupial moles.

8 True or false: A saguaro cactus can live for 200 years.

◆ True

In the Sonoran Desert of North America, these prickly giants can grow as tall as a house!

9 The Gobi Desert stretches over which two countries?

▲ China and Mongolia

In Asia's biggest desert, temperatures can swing wildly between a blazing 122°F (50°C) in the day to –40°F (–40°C) at night. Brrr!

10 Many desert animals are nocturnal. This means they...

● Are most active at night

Desert reptiles, insects, and mammals (like this Fennec fox) hide in the shade until sunset. Then, in the cool evening, they come out to find food.

Podium!

Bronze: 1–5 correct answers
Silver: 6–8 correct answers
Gold: 9–10 correct answers

Forests

Can you see the wood for the trees? Time to see how much you know about Earth's leafiest locations.

1 How much of Earth's land is covered by forest?
- ◆ 10%
- ▲ 30%
- ● 50%

2 Which type of forests are found in warm, wet climates?
- ◆ Tropical rainforests
- ▲ Temperate forests
- ● Coniferous forests

3 What type of forest is a giant panda's ideal habitat?
- ◆ Bamboo forest
- ▲ Mediterranean forest
- ● Pine forest

4 What's the word for the huge, cold forests just south of the Arctic circle?
- ◆ Tundra
- ▲ Taiga
- ● Tonga

Did you know?

In the dense areas of a rainforest, it can take up to 10 minutes for a raindrop to reach the forest floor!

5 Which of these trees is most dangerous to humans?
◆ Manchineel
▲ Giant hogweed
● Man-eating maple

6 Which rainforest monkey is the planet's loudest land animal?
◆ Roarer monkey
▲ Howler monkey
● Boomer monkey

7 This rainforest plant has the world's biggest flower. How big is it?
◆ 2 ft (60 cm) wide
▲ 3 ft 4 in (1.1 m) wide
● 8 ft (2.5 m) wide

8 True or false: Brazil is the country with the largest area of forest on Earth.
◆ True
▲ False

9 The pointed leaves of a conifer tree are called...
◆ Spikes
▲ Pins
● Needles

10 Which body part of a wild boar is ideally adapted to forest living?
◆ Tail
▲ Ears
● Snout

Turn to page 84 for the answers!

Forests
Answers

1 How much of Earth's land is covered by forest?

▲ 30%

That's almost one-third of Earth! The types of forests vary depending on how close they are to the equator and how much rain they get.

2 Which type of forests are found in warm, wet climates?

◆ Tropical rainforests

These hot jungles are found close to Earth's equator. Some parts of the Congo rainforest are so dense that nobody has seen them!

3 What type of forest is a giant panda's ideal habitat?

◆ Bamboo forest

Giant pandas live in the mountains of China, where their main food of bamboo (a tall grass) is abundant.

4 What's the word for the huge, cold forests just south of the Arctic circle?

▲ Taiga

Imagine lots of Christmas trees—that's Taiga! Stretching over northern regions of North America, Russia, and Scandinavia, this forest has fir, spruce, and pine trees.

5 Which of these trees is most dangerous to humans?

◆ Manchineel

This Caribbean tree's applelike fruits are poisonous to humans. Just touching the leaves can cause painful blisters.

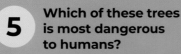

6
Which rainforest monkey is the planet's loudest land animal?

▲ Howler monkey

The male howler's deafening, booming roar can be heard for 3 miles (5 km). It's a warning to others—"Stay away from my tree and my mate!"

7
This rainforest plant has the world's biggest flower. How big is it?

▲ 3 ft 4 in (1.1 m) wide

Rafflesia grows in Southeast Asian rainforests. Its nickname is corpse flower because its bloom stinks, which attracts flies!

8
True or false: Brazil is the country with the largest area of forest on Earth.

▲ False

It's Russia, with more than 19.7 million acres (8 million hectares). Brazil has 12.3 million acres (5 million hectares).

9
The pointed leaves of a conifer tree are called...

● Needles

A conifer's tough, resin-covered spikes don't dry out as easily as wider leaves. This means they can survive hot climates as well as windy, dry Arctic winters.

10
Which body part of a wild boar is ideally adapted to forest living?

● Snout

The boar uses its super-sensitive, snuffly snout to sniff and dig around on the forest floor to find tasty treats like earthworms, fungi, or buried acorns.

Podium!

Bronze: 1–5 correct answers

Silver: 6–8 correct answers

Gold: 9–10 correct answers

Coral Reefs

Slip into your scuba gear and explore a coral reef—it's a multicolored, underwater treasure trove!

1 **What is a coral reef made of?**
- ◆ Animals
- ▲ Plants
- ● Rocks

2 **The world's biggest coral reef is off the coast of...**
- ◆ Australia
- ▲ Jamaica
- ● Japan

4 **What is this coral called?**
- ◆ Maze coral
- ▲ Turtle coral
- ● Brain coral

3 **Coral reefs are usually found in what sort of water?**
- ◆ Deep lakes
- ▲ Warm, shallow seas
- ● Fast-flowing rivers

Did you know?
Corals get their bright colors from the tiny, plantlike algae that live inside their polyps.

5 What is unusual about the Røst coral reef, off the coast of Norway?

◆ It's the oldest reef ever found.

▲ It glows in the dark.

● It grows in cold, deep water.

6 What protects this clown fish from the sea anemone's stinging tentacles?

◆ Jets of water

▲ A layer of slime

● Spiky scales

7 Which of these animals is a major threat to coral reefs?

◆ Crown of thorns starfish

▲ Reef shark

● Box jellyfish

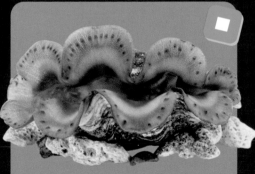

8 True or false: Coral reefs are home to 25 percent of all the world's marine fish species.

◆ True

▲ False

Scan the QR code for a Kahoot! about coral reefs.

9 This monster mollusk weighs up to 660 lb (300 kg) and grows to 4 ft 6 in (1.4 m) long. What's it called?

◆ Olympia oyster

▲ Giant clam

● King sea snail

Turn to page 88 for the answers!

Coral Reefs
Answers

1 What is a coral reef made of?

◆ Animals

Rocklike corals are actually formed by tiny creatures called polyps! Their hard skeletons cling together to make the reef.

2 The world's biggest coral reef is off the coast of...

◆ Australia

The Great Barrier Reef is more than 1,429 miles (2,300 km) long. It can be seen from space by astronauts!

3 Coral reefs are usually found in what sort of water?

▲ Warm, shallow seas

Corals like lots of light and a sea temperature of around 68°F (20°C). Shallow tropical seas are perfect!

4 What is this coral called?

● Brain coral

Like all corals, brain corals don't actually have brains. However, they can live for up to 900 years!

5 What is unusual about the Røst coral reef, off the coast of Norway?

● It grows in cold, deep water

The Røst Reef is made up of Lophelia—the only coral species that can survive in such cold, dark seas.

6 What protects this clown fish from the sea anemone's stinging tentacles?

▲ A layer of slime

These two animals help each other: the clown fish hides from predators among the anemone's tentacles and drops food for the sea anemones to eat—that's teamwork!

7 Which of these animals is a major threat to coral reefs?

◆ Crown of thorns starfish

Swarms of these big, venomous sea stars can quickly munch through a large patch of coral, leaving just bare rock.

8 True or false: Coral reefs are home to 25 percent of all the world's marine fish species.

◆ True

Although coral reefs cover only 1 percent of Earth's surface, they provide a rich habitat to thousands of species of marine life.

9 This monster mollusk weighs up to 660 lb (300 kg) and grows to 4 ft 6 in (1.4 m) long. What's it called?

▲ Giant clam

These reef animals are the heaviest of all mollusks—10,000 times heavier than a garden snail! They can live for 100 years, too.

Podium!

Bronze: 1–5 correct answers

Silver: 6–8 correct answers

Gold: 9–10 correct answers

Grasslands

Where there's not enough rain for a forest, but too much rain for a desert, you'll find grass. Can you pass the grass test?

1 How much of the world's land is covered by grasslands?
◆ About 5%
▲ About 25%
● About 50%

2 What are the two types of grasslands?
◆ Tropical and polar
▲ Temperate and tropical
● Desertified and temperate

4 True or false: The Steppe grasslands are in South America.
◆ True
▲ False

3 What type of animal is the prairie dog?
◆ Rat
▲ Squirrel
● Dog

5 This animal lives in the cerrado grasslands of Brazil. What is it?
◆ Dingo
▲ Giant coyote
● Maned wolf

6 Grassland with some scattered trees is called...

◆ Savanna
▲ Meadow
● Tundra

7 The cowboys who herd cattle on the Pampas of South America are called...

◆ Rancheros
▲ Fritos
● Gauchos

8 What's the biggest animal found on the Rangelands of Northern Australia?

◆ Emu
▲ Dingo
● Red kangaroo

9 How many different species of grasses are there?

◆ 1,500
▲ 4,500
● 11,500

10 Which of these big cats does NOT prowl the African savanna?

◆ Tiger
▲ Lion
● Cheetah

Did you know?
Every year, 2 million wildebeest trek across the savanna of the Serengeti National Park, in search of food. This journey is called the Great Migration.

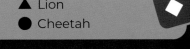

Turn to page 92 for the answers!

Grasslands Answers

1 How much of the world's land is covered by grasslands?

▲ About 25%

Vast plains covered with grasses provide essential food for thousands of species of animals.

2 What are the two types of grasslands?

▲ Temperate and tropical

Temperate grasslands have cold winters and hot summers. Tropical grasslands are hot all year round, with a long dry season.

3 What type of animal is the prairie dog?

▲ Squirrel

These rodents live in burrows under the grasslands of North America, which are called prairies.

4 True or false: The Steppe grasslands are in South America.

▲ False

The Steppe is in Asia. It forms the largest area of grassland in the world. The Pampas are in South America.

5 This animal lives in the cerrado grasslands of Brazil. What is it?

● Maned wolf

The hungry hunter's red fur and long legs have earned it the nickname of "fox on stilts"!

6 Grassland with some scattered trees is called...?

◆ Savanna

In Africa, the Serengeti National Park is dotted with spiky-leaved acacia trees, which only giraffes are tall enough to eat!

7 The cowboys who herd cattle on the Pampas of South America are called...

● Gauchos

Gauchos are skilled nomadic horsemen. They're also prominent in Argentine culture as a symbol of honor, bravery, and freedom.

8 What's the biggest animal found on the Rangelands of Northern Australia?

● Red kangaroo

Adult male roos can be 6 ft 6 in (2 m) tall and can jump 25 ft (7.5 m)—perfect for bouncing over long grass!

9 How many different species of grasses are there?

● 11,500

Grasses grow all over the planet, even on the fringes of Antarctica! They provide food for a range of animals, including humans (we call edible grasses "cereals").

10 Which of these big cats does NOT prowl the African savanna?

◆ Tiger

All of the world's tigers live in Asia. They hunt in many different habitats, including grasslands.

Podium!

Bronze: 1–5 correct answers

Silver: 6–8 correct answers

Gold: 9–10 correct answers

Wetlands

Wade into these testing questions about the soggiest, boggiest habitats on Earth!

1 What are the three main types of wetlands?

◆ Lakes, streams, and puddles
▲ Swamps, marshes, and bogs
● Clay, sand, and soil

2 What are the two main kinds of swamps?

◆ Saltwater and freshwater
▲ Cold water and warm water
● Lowland and highland

3 What's the biggest wetland in the world?

◆ The Sundarbans, India
▲ The Polystovo-Lovatskaya, Europe
● The Pantanal, South America

4 In North American swamps, cypress tree roots that poke out of the water are called...

◆ Elbow roots
▲ Knee roots
● Nose roots

5 The Louisiana Bayous are part of which US river?

◆ Mississippi
▲ Hudson
● Colorado

6 What is the soggy soil of a bog known as?
◆ Coal
▲ Peat
● Loam

7 Can you identify this wetland bird?
◆ Spoonbill
▲ Pelican
● Heron

8 True or false: Saltwater crocodiles can stay underwater for two hours.
◆ True
▲ False

9 Can you identify this water-loving Asian cat?
◆ Marsh cat
▲ Swimming cat
● Fishing cat

Did you know?
Anything buried in bogs can last for thousands of years. Ancient animals, and even humans, have been found perfectly preserved!

10 Which wetland plant has leaves sharp enough to cut cloth?
◆ Knifegrass
▲ Sawgrass
● Bladegrass

Turn to page 96 for the answers!

Wetlands
Answers

1 What are the three main types of wetlands?

▲ Swamps, marshes, and bogs

They're all soaked and spongy, or submerged in shallow water. Marshes and swamps are found in warmer climates than bogs.

2 What are the two main kinds of swamps?

◆ Saltwater and freshwater

Freshwater swamps are inland while saltwater swamps are near the coast. Both have plenty of wildlife.

3 What's the biggest wetland in the world?

● The Pantanal, South America

This mega-marsh covers 66,000 sq miles (171,000 sq km), mostly in Brazil. It's made up of vast grasslands that have been flooded by the Amazon—the world's largest river.

4 In North American swamps, cypress tree roots that poke out of the water are called...

▲ Knee roots

To help the trees survive the waterlogged conditions, these special "knee roots" gather vital oxygen from the air above the water.

5 **The Louisiana Bayous are part of which US river?**
◆ Mississippi
The slow-moving, swampy rivers of the bayous form part of the fan-shaped delta (mouth) of the mighty Mississippi.

6 **What is the soggy soil of a bog known as?**
▲ Peat
This soil, made up of layers of dead plants, forms over thousands of years. In the past, people burned peat to heat their homes.

9 **Can you identify this water-loving Asian cat?**
● Fishing cat
Unlike most cats, this one is totally at home in the water. It even has slightly webbed feet to help it scoop fish out of the water!

7 **Can you identify this wetland bird?**
◆ Spoonbill
This North American bird feeds by swishing its big, sensitive bill through the swampy waters and scooping up lots of shrimp, insects, and fish.

10 **Which wetland plant has leaves sharp enough to cut cloth?**
▲ Sawgrass
This quick-growing marsh plant can grow 9 ft (2.7 m) tall. Its leaves have tiny ridges, like the teeth of a saw, all along its sides.

8 **True or false: Saltwater crocodiles can stay underwater for two hours.**
◆ True
This sneaky swamp-dweller lies still until a prey animal comes close. Then... SNAP! It snatches the animal in its jaws.

Podium!
Bronze: 1–5 correct answers
Silver: 6–8 correct answers
Gold: 9–10 correct answers

Islands

Islands are surrounded by water.
Will these island-themed questions
leave you at all sea?

1 Put these islands
in order of size, with
the largest first.
- ◆ New Guinea
- ▲ Borneo
- ● Greenland

2 Which of these
types of islands is
a ring of coral?
- ◆ Tidal
- ▲ Barrier
- ● Atoll

3 On which US
island would
you find the Empire
State Building?
- ◆ Long Island
- ▲ Manhattan Island
- ● Staten Island

4 The giant tortoise
lives only on
which islands?
- ◆ The Shetlands
- ▲ The Galápagos
- ● The Bahamas

5 Where is the Palm Jumeirah—a human-built island shaped like a palm tree?
◆ India
▲ Morocco
● Dubai

6 The Komodo dragon lives only on islands in which country?
◆ Wales
▲ China
● Indonesia

7 Which of these events can create a new island in the sea?
◆ Asteroid strike
▲ Volcanic eruption
● Shipwreck

8 True or false: An island in the middle of a river (like the Île de la Cité in Paris) is called a rivulet.
◆ True
▲ False

9 One of the most remote uninhabited islands is...
◆ Easter Island
▲ Bouvet Island
● Christmas Island

Did you know?
Surtsey, in Iceland, is one of Earth's youngest islands. It appeared after an undersea volcano erupted in 1963.

Scan the QR code for a Kahoot! about islands.

10 The island nation of Jamaica is surrounded by which sea?
◆ Mediterranean sea
▲ Caribbean sea
● Coral sea

Turn to page 100 for the answers!

Islands
Answers

1 Put these islands in order of size, with the largest first.
- ● Greenland
- ◆ New Guinea
- ▲ Borneo

These are Earth's three biggest islands. Greenland, northeast of Canada, is the largest—it's 1,660 miles (2,670 km) long.

2 Which of these types of islands is a ring of coral?
- ● Atoll

Atolls are mainly found in the Pacific and Indian Oceans. A rocky coral circle (reef) surrounds shallow water called a lagoon.

3 On which US island would you find the Empire State Building?
- ▲ Manhattan Island

Manhattan is one of the five boroughs that make up New York City. The Bronx is the only borough that isn't on an island.

4 The giant tortoise lives only on which islands?
- ▲ The Galápagos

These islands, off the coast of South America, are so isolated that they've evolved some unique species. The giant tortoise can be 5 ft (1.5 m) long and weigh 500 lb (225 kg)!

5 Where is the Palm Jumeirah—a human-built island shaped like a palm tree?

● Dubai

Sand from the desert and the seabed helped create this artificial island. It's home to top luxury hotels.

6 The Komodo dragon lives only on islands in which country?

● Indonesia

They're found on only five islands, including Komodo, the island that they're named after.

7 Which of these events can create a new island in the sea?

▲ Volcanic eruption

When an underwater volcano erupts, lava pours into the water, where it cools and solidifies into an island of rock.

8 True or false: An island in the middle of a river (like the Île de la Cité in Paris) is called a rivulet.

▲ False

It's called either "eyot" or "ait"—you say both like the number "eight." A rivulet is a stream.

9 One of the most remote uninhabited islands is...

▲ Bouvet Island

This area of ice and rock is 1,500 miles (2,400 km) south of Africa and 1,000 miles (1,600 km) north of Antarctica.

10 The island nation of Jamaica is surrounded by which sea?

▲ Caribbean sea

Including Jamaica, more than 700 volcanic islands sit between the warm, tropical waters of the Caribbean Sea and the Atlantic Ocean.

Podium!

Bronze: 1–5 correct answers
Silver: 6–8 correct answers
Gold: 9–10 correct answers

Polar Regions

Earth's North and South Poles are remote, bleak, and very cold! What do you know about our planet's frozen places?

1 Which polar region is the coldest?
- ◆ The Arctic (around the North Pole)
- ▲ The Antarctic (around the South Pole)

2 Can you name this heavyweight Arctic resident?
- ◆ Elephant seal
- ▲ Walrus
- ● Narwhal

3 This Arctic dog is a...
- ◆ St. Bernard
- ▲ Newfoundland
- ● Husky

4 The largest city within the Arctic Circle is...
- ◆ Murmansk, Russia
- ▲ Tromso, Norway
- ● Rovaniemi, Finland

5 True or false: No humans live at the South Pole.
- ◆ True
- ▲ False

6 True or false: It's too cold for volcanoes in the polar regions.
◆ True
▲ False

7 Which explorer was the first to reach the South Pole?
◆ Roald Amundsen
▲ Robert Scott
● Christopher Columbus

8 Which Arctic whale can break through sea ice that's 8 in (20 cm) thick?
◆ Blue whale
▲ Orca
● Bowhead whale

9 Which Arctic people build igloos to shelter in?
◆ Inuit
▲ Sami
● Dolgan

10 How does an emperor penguin look after an egg before the chick hatches?
◆ It buries the egg in the snow.
▲ It balances the egg on its feet.
● It builds a nest from its feathers.

Turn to page 104 for the answers!

Polar Regions
Answers

1 **Which polar region is the coldest?**

▲ The Antarctic (around the South Pole)

The continent of Antarctica is Earth's coldest place. The average temperature is –58°F (–50°C), but it can reach –135°F (–93°C)!

2 **Can you name this heavyweight Arctic resident?**

▲ Walrus

These huge mammals can be 10 ft (3 m) long. The males use their tusks to fight and to get out of the water.

3 **This Arctic dog is a...**

● Husky

This Siberian breed is a close relative of the gray wolf. With its strength and stamina, it's often used to pull sledges across the ice.

4 **The largest city within the Arctic Circle is...**

◆ Murmansk, Russia

About 300,000 people live in this fishing port. Its deep, ice-free harbor makes it popular with ships.

5 **True or false: No humans live at the South Pole.**

▲ False

About 150 scientists live there, although some go home in winter! They live at the Amundsen-Scott Station—an American research center that opened in 1957.

6 **True or false: It's too cold for volcanoes in the polar regions.**

▲ False

Antarctica has hundreds of volcanoes! Mount Erebus is one of the most active volcanoes on Earth.

9 **Which Arctic people build igloos to shelter in?**

◆ Inuit

The Inuit people build these temporary shelters with blocks of packed snow. The air trapped in the snow is a good insulator, making the igloos really cozy!

10 **How does an emperor penguin look after an egg before the chick hatches?**

▲ It balances the egg on its feet.

The male emperor is responsible for incubating the egg. He warms it under a flap of skin on his belly and uses his feet to keep it off the ice.

7 **Which explorer was the first to reach the South Pole?**

◆ Roald Amundsen

Amundsen and his team reached the South Pole on December 14, 1912. They beat the British group, led by Robert Scott, by 34 days!

8 **Which Arctic whale can break through sea ice that's 8 in (20 cm) thick?**

● Bowhead whale

Its extra-thick skull helps this predator break through the sea ice to breathe. Its very thick blubber helps it survive the icy waters.

Podium!

Bronze: 1–5 correct answers
Silver: 6–8 correct answers
Gold: 9–10 correct answers

Cities

Build up your knowledge of cities with these questions, and you'll soon be streets ahead of everyone!

1 True or False: Oslo in Norway is the world's most northerly capital city.
◆ True
▲ False

2 A megacity is a city with a population of more than...
◆ 5 million people
▲ 10 million people
● 20 million people

3 What was the name of the world's first-ever big city?
◆ Uruk
▲ Babylon
● London

4 The Little Mermaid sculpture sits in the harbor of which European city?
◆ Copenhagen, Denmark
▲ Stockholm, Sweden
● Oslo, Norway

Did you know?
Brazil's capital, Brasilia, was built in 1960 and was laid out so that from the air, it looks like an airplane!

5 The Pyramids of Giza are on the outskirts of which African city?
◆ Alexandria
▲ Khartoum
● Cairo

6 How many capital cities does South Africa have?
- ◆ None
- ▲ One
- ● Three

7 Washington, DC, is the capital of the US, but what was the country's first capital city?
- ◆ New York City
- ▲ Philadelphia
- ● Chicago

8 Africa's biggest city, Lagos, is in which country?
- ◆ Egypt
- ▲ Nigeria
- ● Morocco

9 The ancient city of Machu Picchu was built by which people?
- ◆ Aztec
- ▲ Inca
- ● Māori

10 Which Italian city surrounds a tiny independent country?
- ◆ Venice
- ▲ Rome
- ● Milan

Scan the QR code for a Kahoot! about cities.

Turn to page 108 for the answers!

Cities

Answers

1 True or False: Oslo in Norway is the world's most northerly capital city.

▲ False

Reykjavík in Iceland is the capital that's farthest north—it's just 1,789 miles (2,879 km) from the North Pole.

2 A megacity is a city with a population of more than...

▲ 10 million people

In 1950, New York was the only megacity in the world. In 2023, there were nearly 50, and the total is rising!

3 What was the name of the world's first-ever big city?

◆ Uruk

Cities first sprung up in Mesopotamia—a farming region that's now part of Iraq. In 2,900 BCE, Uruk may have had more than 50,000 residents.

4 The Little Mermaid sculpture sits in the harbor of which European city?

◆ Copenhagen, Denmark

The Little Mermaid is a famous fairytale by Danish writer Hans Christian Andersen.

5 The Pyramids of Giza are on the outskirts of which African city?

● Cairo

These huge stone pyramids were built by the ancient Egyptians as tombs for their rulers, the pharaohs.

6 How many capital cities does South Africa have?

● Three

Most countries have one capital, but South Africa has three: Cape Town, where the National Parliament sits; Pretoria, home of the president; and Bloemfontein, where the legal system is based.

7 Washington, DC, is the capital of the US, but what was the country's first capital city?

▲ Philadelphia

After the US won independence from Britain, Philadelphia served as the new nation's capital for 10 years from 1790. In 1800, the specially built city of Washington took over the job.

8 Africa's biggest city, Lagos, is in which country?

▲ Nigeria

In 2023, 15.9 million people called Lagos home. The city has grown since 1990, when its population was only 4 million!

9 The ancient city of Machu Picchu was built by which people?

▲ Inca

The Incas were skilled farmers and builders, who lived in the Andes mountains of South America, almost 600 years ago. Machu Picchu was abandoned when European invaders defeated the Inca emperor in 1532.

10 Which Italian city surrounds a tiny independent country?

▲ Rome

In the heart of Rome is the Vatican City, home of the Pope and the world's smallest state. At just 0.17 sq miles (0.44 sq km), you could walk around the whole country in an hour!

Podium!

Bronze: 1–5 correct answers
Silver: 6–8 correct answers
Gold: 9–10 correct answers

Record Breakers

Take a tour of our planet and discover its record-breaking wonders, from the tallest to the deepest, and more!

1 The world's highest waterfall is called...?
- ◆ Heaven Falls
- ▲ Fairy Falls
- ● Angel Falls

2 Which two countries share the longest border in the world?
- ◆ China and Russia
- ▲ US and Canada
- ● Brazil and Bolivia

3 The world's busiest train station is in which city?
- ◆ Tokyo, Japan
- ▲ New York, US
- ● Moscow, Russia

4 Which two US states have the most and the least people?
- ◆ Texas and Alaska
- ▲ Florida and North Dakota
- ● California and Wyoming

Did you know?
The heaviest eggplant was grown in the UK in 2021. It weighed a huge 6 lb 14 oz (3.12 kg)!

5 Put the three longest rivers in Asia in order, starting with the longest:
- ◆ Mekong River
- ▲ Yellow River
- ● Yangtze River

6 Which hurricane caused $125 billion worth of damage, making it the most expensive in history?
- ◆ Hurricane Andrew, 1992
- ▲ Hurricane Ida, 2022
- ● Hurricane Katrina, 2005

7 This is the tallest bridge in the world. In which country can you find it?
- ◆ Argentina
- ▲ France
- ● South Africa

8 The world's largest meteorite crater we know about is in...
- ◆ South Africa
- ▲ Mexico
- ● Germany

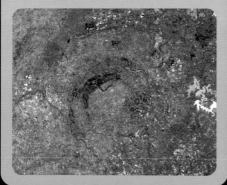

9 Which animal is the Amazon rainforest's most venomous?
- ◆ Giant centipede
- ▲ Banana spider
- ● Golden poison dart frog

Turn to page 112 for the answers!

Record Breakers
Answers

1 **The world's highest waterfall is called...?**
● Angel Falls
High in the remote mountains of Venezuela, the spectacular Angel Falls is 3,212 ft (979 m) high—more than twice as tall as New York's Empire State Building.

2 **Which two countries share the longest border in the world?**

▲ US and Canada
The border between these two huge North American countries is 5,524 miles (8,890 km) long. Part of the border is made up of the famous Niagara Falls (pictured).

4 **Which two US states have the most and the least people?**
● California and Wyoming
California has the largest US population with approximately 39 million people. Although it's the 10th largest state by area, Wyoming has only over half a million residents!

3 **The world's busiest train station is in which city?**
◆ Tokyo, Japan
More than 3.6 million people pass through Tokyo's Shinjuku Station every day!

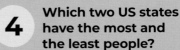

5 Put the three longest rivers in Asia in order, starting with the longest:

- ● Yangtze River
- ▲ Yellow River
- ◆ Mekong River

The Yangtze flows 3,900 miles (6,300 km) across China. The Yellow River is Earth's muddiest. The Mekong River flows through six countries.

6 Which hurricane caused $125 billion worth of damage, making it the most expensive in history?

- ● Hurricane Katrina, 2005

Hurricane Katrina left 1 million people homeless and 5 million without any power. More than 1,800 people lost their lives.

7 This is the tallest ~~bridge in the world~~. In which country can you find it?

- ▲ France

The Millau Viaduct in southern France crosses the valley of the Tarn River to connect the city of Montpelier to Paris. Its tallest mast is 1,125 ft (343 m) high!

8 The world's largest meteorite crater we know about is in...

- ◆ South Africa

The Vredefort crater is the result of a huge space rock crashing into Earth 2 billion years ago. Its edges have been eroded, but the crater could be up to 186 miles (300 km) wide.

9 Which animal is the Amazon rainforest's most venomous?

- ● Golden poison dart frog

All three of these animals are poisonous, but the golden poison dart frog has the most venom. One frog has enough to kill 10 humans!

Podium!

Bronze: 1–5 correct answers
Silver: 6–8 correct answers
Gold: 9–10 correct answers

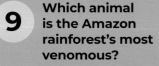

Farming

Get your Wellingtons on and get the low down on sowing, growing, mowing—and everything else farmers do to feed the world!

1 The word "agriculture" comes from the Greek word for...
- ◆ Farmer
- ▲ Field
- ● Goat

2 A farm that grows only crops (plants grown for food) is called...
- ◆ A dairy farm
- ▲ An arable farm
- ● A pastoral farm

3 True or false: One-third of all the food produced by farmers is wasted.
- ◆ True
- ▲ False

4 What type of farm animal is a Gloucester Old Spot?
- ◆ Cow
- ▲ Pig
- ● Chicken

5 What is aquaculture?
- ◆ Growing vegetables underwater
- ▲ Fish farming
- ● Watering crops with seawater

Did you know?
It takes around 660 gallons (2,500 liters) of water to grow just 2 lb 3 oz (1 kg) of rice!

6 Can you name this animal, farmed for its extra-soft, fine wool?

◆ Kashmir goat
▲ Mongolian sheep
● Alpaca

7 Put these crops in order, starting with the tallest:

◆ Corn
▲ Sugar cane
● Wheat
■ Rice

8 Which part of the tea plant is used to make tea, the world's favorite drink?

◆ Leaves
▲ Root
● Stems

9 Which animal's milk is traditionally used to make mozzarella cheese?

◆ Goat
▲ Cow
● Buffalo

10 True or false: More apples are produced and eaten than any other fruit.

◆ True
▲ False

 Turn to page 116 for the answers!

Farming
Answers

1 The word "agriculture" comes from the Greek word for...

▲ Field

Agriculture is farming—Earth's oldest human job! The first farmers planted crops in fields to feed themselves and their families.

2 A farm that grows only crops (plants grown for food) is called...

▲ An arable farm

Where arable crops are grown depends on the land and climate. Flat fields are good for wheat, while hills are best for rice.

3 True or false: One-third of all the food produced by farmers is wasted.

◆ True

Every year, around 1.3 billion tons of food is wasted! Farmers can't always keep food fresh until it reaches customers. Also, sometimes in developed countries food is bought and not eaten.

4 What type of farm animal is a Gloucester Old Spot?

▲ Pig

This ancient breed of pig is sometimes called the orchard pig because it eats fallen apples off the ground.

5 What is aquaculture?

▲ Fish farming

Some fish can be raised on fish farms. Half of all the fish we eat is farmed in underwater cages. The fish are looked after, just like farm animals on land.

6
Can you name this animal, farmed for its extra-soft, fine wool?

● Alpaca

Originally from the Andes mountains in South America, woolly alpacas are the fleeciest members of the llama family.

8
Which part of the tea plant is used to make tea, the world's favorite drink?

◆ Leaves

For the best tea, skilled pickers pluck only the most tender leaves from the tops of evergreen tea plants.

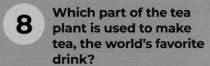

7
Put these crops in order, starting with the tallest:

▲ Sugar cane
◆ Corn
■ Rice
● Wheat

Sugar cane is a very tall grass with a thick stem called a cane. The cane's sweet juice can be turned into the sugar that we use at home, as well as animal feed and even fuel for cars!

9
Which animal's milk is traditionally used to make mozzarella cheese?

● Buffalo

No pizza is complete without a bubbling, tangy topping of mozzarella! Buffalo milk is thicker and creamier than cow's milk, making it especially good for cheese making.

10
True or false: More apples are produced and eaten than any other fruit.

▲ False

Apples are only third in the league table of fruits; watermelons come second and the top spot goes to... bananas!

Podium!

Bronze: 1–5 correct answers
Silver: 6–8 correct answers
Gold: 9–10 correct answers

Human Earth

Humans have transformed the Earth in our mission to build homes, travel, and make the items we need or want.

1 True or false: The world population is growing by around 70 million people every year.
- ◆ True
- ▲ False

2 The Mponeng mine is the world's deepest. Which metal is mined there?
- ◆ Silver
- ▲ Gold
- ● Lead

3 Which is the most crowded country in the world?
- ◆ China
- ▲ Mexico
- ● Monaco

Did you know?
The US has the world's biggest road network, with more than 4.2 million miles (6.8 million km) of drivable roads.

4 This building gets more visitors than any other. Where is it?
- ◆ Beijing, China
- ▲ Tokyo, Japan
- ● Las Vegas, US

5 Coal and gas are called "fossil fuels" because...

◆ They developed from the remains of animals and plants

▲ They developed in the time of the dinosaurs

● They are an old-fashioned form of energy.

6 True or false: Earth is constantly making new fossil fuels for us to extract and use.

◆ True

▲ False

7 The Trans-Siberian railroad runs between...

◆ Moscow and Vladivostok in Russia

▲ Vienna in Austria and Beijing in China

● Kiev in Ukraine and Ulan Bator, Mongolia

8 Japan's Shinkansen is the world's fastest train. What is its nickname?

◆ Bullet train

▲ Lightning train

● Rocket train

9 True or false: 10 percent of people in the world don't have access to the internet.

◆ True

▲ False

10 Which country has the tallest men in the world, on average?

◆ US

▲ Netherlands

● Argentina

Turn to page 120 for the answers!

Human Earth

Answers

1 True or false: The world population is growing by around 70 million people every year.

◆ True

More than 8 billion people live on Earth. The total is still slowly increasing by 1 percent each year.

2 The Mponeng mine is the world's deepest. Which metal is mined there?

▲ Gold

This South African gold mine is more than 2.5 miles (4 km) deep! Slushy ice is pumped down to keep the miners cool.

3 Which is the most crowded country in the world?

● Monaco

It has fewer people than China or Mexico, but Monaco's 40,000 people are crammed into 0.77 sq miles (2 sq km), making it the most crowded place.

4 This building gets more visitors than any other. Where is it?

◆ Beijing, China

The Forbidden City is a massive walled palace complex built by the Chinese Yongle Emperor in the early 1400s.

5 Coal and gas are called "fossil fuels" because...

◆ They developed from the remains of animals and plants.

Extracting and burning fossil fuels is harming the environment, so we need to find cleaner energy sources.

6

True or false: Earth is constantly making new fossil fuels for us to extract and use.

▲ False

Earth takes hundreds of millions of years to make fossil fuels, which is too slow for us to keep using. Once the fuel is used up there won't be any more!

7

The Trans-Siberian railroad runs between...

◆ Moscow and Vladivostok in Russia

This rail trip—the world's longest without changing trains—takes eight days and covers 5,766 miles (9,279 km).

8

Japan's Shinkansen is the world's fastest train. What is its nickname?

◆ Bullet train

These electric trains run on specially designed tracks at 200 mph (320 km/h).

9

True or false: 10 percent of people in the world don't have access to the internet.

▲ False

In fact, almost 3 billion people—more than a third of all humans—aren't online at all. Most of the people without internet access are in developing countries, especially in rural or poorer areas.

10

Which country has the tallest men in the world, on average?

▲ Netherlands

An average Dutch man's height is 5 ft 11 in (182.54 cm). The Netherlands doesn't have the tallest women, though—that title belongs to Latvia, where women average 5 ft 7 in (169.8 cm).

Podium!

Bronze: 1–5 correct answers

Silver: 6–8 correct answers

Gold: 9–10 correct answers

Endangered Earth

Our planet is precious! How much do you know about the risks Earth faces and how to keep it safe for the future?

1 True or false: Earth is warming up quicker than ever before.
◆ True
▲ False

2 What is the greenhouse effect?
◆ When gases trap heat in our atmosphere and warm up Earth
▲ When polar ice melts in the summer
● When fertilizers are used to make crops grow better

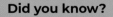

3 The world's biggest landfill site is in which country?
◆ Germany
▲ US
● South Korea

4 Which of these is NOT a form of renewable energy?
◆ Solar power
▲ Wind power
● Natural gas

Did you know?

More than 9,000 animal species are in critical danger of extinction, according to the International Union for Conservation of Nature (IUCN).

5 What are tiny fragments of broken-down plastic in the ocean called?
- ◆ Nanoplastics
- ▲ Megaplastics
- ● Microplastics

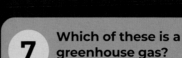

6 How long can it take for one plastic water bottle to break down?
- ◆ Up to 10 years
- ▲ Up to 150 years
- ● Up to 450 years

7 Which of these is a greenhouse gas?
- ◆ Oxygen
- ▲ Hydrogen
- ● Carbon dioxide

8 True or false: You can recycle glass an unlimited number of times.
- ◆ True
- ▲ False

9 Can you identify this endangered animal?
- ◆ Amur leopard
- ▲ Cheetah
- ● Bobcat

Turn to page 124 for the answers!

Endangered Earth
Answers

1 True or false: Earth is warming up quicker than ever before.

◆ True

Human activities, like burning fossil fuels, have changed our atmosphere and caused temperatures to rise. This is affecting Earth's climate and life on land and in the oceans.

2 What is the greenhouse effect?

◆ When gases trap heat in our atmosphere and warm up Earth

Greenhouse gases act like a blanket, keeping Earth warm enough for us to survive. However, too much greenhouse gas means Earth gets too warm, posing a risk to life on our planet.

3 The world's biggest landfill site is in which country?

▲ US

The world's biggest landfill is in Las Vegas, Nevada. It covers 2,200 acres (890 hectares).

4 Which of these is NOT a form of renewable energy?

● Natural gas

As it's a fossil fuel, natural gas isn't renewable: once used, it's gone forever. However, solar energy is renewable. Solar panels collect sunlight and turn it into power.

5 **What are tiny fragments of broken-down plastic in the ocean called?**

● Microplastics

When sunlight and waves act on plastic objects in the ocean, the plastic breaks into very tiny fragments. These microplastics can be very harmful to ocean animals if they eat them by mistake.

6 **How long can it take for one plastic water bottle to break down?**

● Up to 450 years

If you buy a bottle of water today, it could still be around in 450 years! Even when it finally breaks down into microplastics, those tiny fragments will stay on our planet forever. Best to use a reusable water bottle.

7 **Which of these is a greenhouse gas?**

● Carbon dioxide

Carbon dioxide (CO_2) is one of the three main greenhouse gases. They are a natural part of our atmosphere, but human activities have raised their levels, causing the greenhouse effect.

8 **True or false: You can recycle glass an unlimited number of times.**

◆ True

Glass can be made into something new again and again without it losing any quality. Plastic is different, though; it can be recycled only about three times before its quality decreases.

9 **Can you identify this endangered animal?**

◆ Amur leopard

Only about 100 of these Asian leopards are left in the wild. They're now endangered because of humans' actions, such as building on the leopards' habitats and hunting them for fur.

Podium!

Bronze: 1–5 correct answers

Silver: 6–8 correct answers

Gold: 9–10 correct answers

Glossary

Climate
The average, normal weather conditions in a particular area over a long period of time.

Colony
A group of animals of the same species that live together.

Crater
A bowl-shaped hollow in Earth's surface, often formed by an impact or an explosion, such as a volcanic eruption.

Equator
An imaginary line running around the widest part of Earth. It is an equal distance from the North and South poles.

Evaporation
When water turns from a liquid to a gas (water vapor), usually by being heated.

Magnetic field
The area around a magnet where the magnetic force will work. Within the field, magnetic force can either pull two magnets together or push them apart.

Magnitude
The term used to describe the strength of an earthquake. It's measured in different ways, including the Mercalli Scale.

Organisms
Any living things, from bacteria and fungi to more complex life forms such as plants and animals.

Particles
Extremely small units, such as atoms or molecules, that make up a solid, liquid, or gas.

Pollution
The dumping of waste or harmful materials into the environment, causing damage to rivers, land, or the atmosphere.

Rift
A widening gap created by rocks or the plates of Earth's crust pulling apart.

Solar system
The sun and the planets, moons, asteroids, and all other space bodies that orbit it and are held by its gravity.

Tectonic plates
Large, slow-moving pieces of rock that make up Earth's outer layer called the crust.

Picture Credits

The publisher would like to thank the following for their kind permission to reproduce their photographs:

(Key: a-above; b-below/bottom; c-center; f-far; l-left; r-right; t-top)

2 123RF.com: Leonello Calvetti (bl). Getty Images / iStock: bobainsworth (cra). 3 Dorling Kindersley: Wildlife Heritage Foundation, Kent, UK (bl). Dreamstime.com: Dennis Donohue / Silksatsunrise (tr). 4 Dorling Kindersley: Will Heap / John Pitt (cr). Dreamstime.com: Matthijs Kuijpers / Mgkuijpers (bl). 6 123RF.com: 1xpert (cra). 7 Getty Images: Mike Hill (bl). 9 Dreamstime.com: Solarseven (bl). 10 Dorling Kindersley: Gary Ombler / Senckenberg Gesellschaft Fuer Naturforschung Museum (bl). 11 Dorling Kindersley: Colin Keates / Natural History Museum, London (tr). Getty Images / iStock: bobainsworth (crb). 12 Dreamstime.com: Emoke Kupai (cr). 13 123RF.com: Sayompu Chamnankit (clb). 14 Dreamstime.com: Patrick Evans (crb); Oksanaphoto (bl). 15 Alamy Stock Photo: Operation 2022 (cr). Shutterstock.com: Ppito00 (bl). 16 Getty Images / iStock: zetter (clb). 17 123RF.com: saiko3p (tr). Dorling Kindersley: Andy and Gill Swash (bl). 18 Dreamstime.com: Brian Kushner (clb). Ed Merritt / Dorling Kindersley: Merritt Cartographic (cra). 19 123RF.com: Amy Harris (cra). Dreamstime.com: Sailorr (clb). 20 123RF.com: Galyna Andrushko (clb); Sean Pavone (crb). Getty Images / iStock: nicolamargaret (cra). 22 Dreamstime.com: Yekaixp (cra). 23 Dreamstime.com: Tom Wang / Tomwang112 (tr); Wisconsinart (bl). 24 Dreamstime.com: Oriontrail (cra). 25 123RF.com: Kelly Headrick (clb). 26 Dreamstime.com: Sergii Kolesnyk (cra). Getty Images / iStock: Jennifer_Sharp (bl). 27 Dreamstime.com: Bojan Dimic (cla). 28 Dreamstime.com: Olgacov (cra). 29 Dorling Kindersley: Christopher Pillitz (clb). 30 Dorling Kindersley: Will Heap / John Pitt (bl). Dreamstime.com: Gillian Hardy (tr). 31 Dreamstime.com: Hotshotsworldwide (cra). 32 Getty Images: Peter Unger (cl). 33 Dreamstime.com: Mark Higgins / Markrhiggins (clb). 34 Dreamstime.com: Andrea Willmore (br). 35 Dreamstime.com: Anthony Hathaway / F2 (cra); Raymond Kasprzak / Rkasprzak (clb). 36 123RF.com: Roman Lysogor (br). Dreamstime.com: Daniel Prudek (cra). 37 Dreamstime.com: Andrey Gudkov (br). 38 Getty Images: Jim Sugar (cl). 39 Dorling Kindersley: NASA / JPL (clb). Getty Images / iStock: shirophoto (cra). 40 Dreamstime.com: Tamara Kulikova (bl). 41 Alamy Stock Photo: imageBROKER.com GmbH & Co. KG / Josef Beck (cla). Science Photo Library: David Weintraub (cr). 43 Dreamstime.com: Suranga Weeratunga (cra). Getty Images: Kirsten Boos / EyeEm (tr). 44 Dreamstime.com: Bennymarty (cra). 45 Dreamstime.com: Luckyphotographer (tl). Getty Images / iStock: rusm (cr). 46 Dreamstime.com: Yehuda Bernstein (bl). Getty Images / iStock: AndreaWillmore (cra). 47 Dreamstime.com: Jiawangkun (crb). 48 Dorling Kindersley: David Peart (crb). 49 Alamy Stock Photo: Design Pics / Radius Images (bl). 50 Fotolia: apttone (br). Shutterstock.com: Yes058 Montree (c). 51 Dorling Kindersley: Richard Leeney / Holts Gems, Hatton Garden (cl); Gary Ombler, Oxford University Museum of Natural History (c). Dreamstime.com: Ron Sumners / Sumnersgraphicsinc (tr). 52 Dreamstime.com: Vera Golovina (bl). 53 Getty Images / iStock: benedek (cra). 54 Dreamstime.com: Andrey Gudkov (crb). 56 Dreamstime.com: Iuliia Kuzenkova (cra). 57 Dreamstime.com: Hotshotsworldwide (br). 58 Getty Images / iStock: mtnmichelle (crb). 59 Dreamstime.com: Sergey Uryadnikov / Surz01 (cr); Vladimir Melnik / Zanskar (bl). 60 Dreamstime.com: Checco (bl). 61 Alamy Stock Photo: Archive PL (bl). 62 123RF.com: Leonello Calvetti (cra). 63 Dreamstime.com: John A. Anderson / Johnandersonphoto (tr); Manjik (bl). 64 Dreamstime.com: Izanbar (br). 65 Alamy Stock Photo: The History Collection (cla). 66 123RF.com: Nataliia Kravchuk (cra). Getty Images / iStock: ErmakovaElena (bl). 67 Dreamstime.com: Arsty (clb). Getty Images / iStock: mdesigner125 (tr). 68 Dreamstime.com: Rudy Umans (clb). 69 Dreamstime.com: Adonis Villanueva / Adonis84 (tr). Getty Images: Wei Hao Ho (crb). 70 Dreamstime.com: Ryan Deberardinis (bl); Justin Hobson (crb). 71 Dreamstime.com: Akinshin (clb). 72 Getty Images: Beau Van Der Graaf / EyeEm (cr). 73 Alamy Stock Photo: Associated Press / Anastasia Gruzdeva (bl). 74 Getty Images / iStock: gustavofrazao (cra). 75 Dreamstime.com: Kungverylucky (bl); Dennis Donohue / Silksatsunrise (tr). 76 Dreamstime.com: Rinus Baak / Rinusbaak (cr). 77 Dreamstime.com: Ronnachai Limpakdeesavasd (bl). 78 Dreamstime.com: Kairi Aun (cra). Getty Images / iStock: Ron and Patty Thomas (br). 79 Dreamstime.com: Dmitry Pichugin (cra). Getty Images: Thomas Roche (cl). 80 123RF.com: Nataliya Hora (cra). 81 Dreamstime.com: Tzooka (bl). 82 Alamy Stock Photo: SCPhotos / Dallas,John Heaton (bl). Dreamstime.com: Tt (cr). 83 Dreamstime.com: Bokgallery (cl). 84 Alamy Stock Photo: SPP Images (br). 86 123RF.com: Volodymyr Golubyev (cra). Dreamstime.com: Deborah Coles (br). 87 Dreamstime.com: Jamiegodson (cra). 88 Alamy Stock Photo: NASA Image Collection (crb). 89 Getty Images / iStock: tae208 (cra). 90 Dorling Kindersley: Gary Ombler / Cotswold Wildlife Park (cl). Dreamstime.com: Anankkml (br). 91 Getty Images / iStock: pierivb (cr). Shutterstock.com: buteo (cl). 92 Dreamstime.com: Longtaildog (cra). 95 Dreamstime.com: Lukas Blazek / Lukyslukys (bl); Steve Byland / Stevebyland (cra). 96 123RF.com: yobro10 (crb). 98 123RF.com: Yongyut Kumsri (cra); Robert McIntyre (cl); smileus (br). 99 Dreamstime.com: Blagodeyatel (cra). 100 Getty Images / iStock: Snowshill (cl). 102 Dreamstime.com: Dmitry Kalinovsky / Kadmy (clb); Vladimir Seliverstov / Vladsilver (cr); Darryn Schneider (br). 103 123RF.com: ivan kmit / smit (bl). Getty Images / iStock: KeithSzafranski (cr). 104 123RF.com: Witold Kaszkin (cra). 105 Dreamstime.com: Martyn Unsworth (cla). 106 Dreamstime.com: Onefivenine (cra). 107 Dreamstime.com: Jarnogz (cra); Kasto80 (clb). 108 Dreamstime.com: Jeremyreds (cra). 110 Dreamstime.com: Macbibi (clb). 111 Alamy Stock Photo: Universal Images Group North America LLC / Planet Observer (bl). 112 Dreamstime.com: Erix2005 (cra). 113 Dreamstime.com: Matthijs Kuijpers / Mgkuijpers (bl). 114 Dreamstime.com: Stockr (cra). 115 Getty Images / iStock: Gannet77 (cr). 116 Dreamstime.com: Ian Allenden (cra). 117 Getty Images / iStock: Masuti (clb). 118 Dreamstime.com: Jingaiping (br). Getty Images / iStock: AnilSharma55 (cl). 119 Dreamstime.com: Sirikornt (crb). 120 Dreamstime.com: Rudi1976 (br). 121 Dreamstime.com: Sean Pavone (bl). 122 Dreamstime.com: Vchalup (cb). 123 123RF.com: bbtreesubmission (cb). Dorling Kindersley: Wildlife Heritage Foundation, Kent, UK (bl). Getty Images / iStock: AFransen (cr); imv (tr). 124 Dreamstime.com: Broker (br). 126 Dorling Kindersley: Richard Leeney / Holts Gems, Hatton Garden (bc). Fotolia: apttone (br). 127 Dorling Kindersley: Colin Keates / Natural History Museum, London (clb). 128 Dreamstime.com: Rinus Baak / Rinusbaak (tr); Sergey Uryadnikov / Surz01 (bl). Getty Images / iStock: Masuti (br).

Cover images: Front: 123RF.com: Leonello Calvetti br; Dorling Kindersley: Wildlife Heritage Foundation, Kent, UK clb; Back: 123RF.com: smileus cl; Dreamstime.com: Rinus Baak / Rinusbaak tl; Fotolia: apttone tr

All other images © Dorling Kindersley

Dorling Kindersley would like to thank Morten Versvik, Ritesh Maisuria, Perla P. Pinto, Francisco Bembibre, and Craig Narveson at Kahoot! DK also thanks the author Rona Skene; James McKeag for design assistance; consultant David Holmes for fact checking; and Elizabeth Dowsett for proofreading.

DK Penguin Random House

DK LONDON

Senior Editor Laura Palosuo
Senior Art Editor Anna Formanek
Editor Elizabeth Cook
US Senior Editor Jennette ElNaggar
Designer Samantha Richiardi
Consultant David Holmes
Managing Editor Paula Regan
Managing Art Editor Jo Connor
Managing Director Mark Searle
Senior Production Editor Jennifer Murray
Senior Production Controller Lloyd Robertson
Jacket Designers James McKeag
and Samantha Richiardi
Written by Rona Skene

First American Edition, 2024
Published in the United States by DK Publishing
a division of Penguin Random House LLC
1745 Broadway, 20th Floor, New York, NY 10019

Page copyright design © 2024 Dorling Kindersley Limited
A Penguin Random House Company

Kahoot! and the K! logo are
trademarks of Kahoot! ASA.
Copyright ©2024, Kahoot!
All rights reserved.

24 25 26 27 28 10 9 8 7 6 5 4 3 2 1
001– 340622–June/2024

All rights reserved.
Without limiting the rights under the copyright reserved above, no part of this
publication may be reproduced, stored in or introduced into a retrieval system,
or transmitted, in any form, or by any means (electronic, mechanical,
photocopying, recording, or otherwise), without the prior written
permission of the copyright owner.
Published in Great Britain by Dorling Kindersley Limited

A catalog record for this book
is available from the Library of Congress.
ISBN 978-0-7440-9894-5

Printed and bound in China

www.dk.com
www.kahoot.com
create.kahoot.it/profiles/dk-learning-uk

MIX
Paper | Supporting
responsible forestry
FSC™ C018179

This book was made with Forest
Stewardship Council™ certified
paper—one small step in DK's
commitment to a sustainable future.
Learn more at
www.dk.com/uk/information/sustainability